Introduction to Office Software:

Word – Excel – PowerPoint – Paint

By:

Darrell W. Hajek

Cover

Other books by Darrell Hajek

Computer textbooks:

Introduction to Computer Graphics

Introduction to LibreOffice Productivity Software:

Writer – Calc – Impress

Introduction to Computers

(With Cesar Herrera)

Principles of Operating Systems

(With Cesar Herrera)

Fiction/Fantasy:

The Life and Times of Harry Wolf

This book is intended for students with little or no experience in using computers. It introduces the concept of a file, then describes how to utilize and navigate a file storage system and the Internet. It gives brief descriptions (with examples) of how to use the basic Microsoft productivity applications: Notepad, Word, Excel and PowerPoint. A section on Microsoft Paint is also included, since these productivity programs include the ability to insert graphics and some basic graphics editing capabilities will be useful for people using them.

It was written primarily in response to the increasing prices of the texts being used in computer literacy courses. (The prices had increased to the point where students actively resisted purchasing them.) Another factor was the deteriorating support provided by the companies publishing those texts.

The book is intended as an introductory text, not a reference manual. The idea is to give a beginning student enough tools to make the programs useful. After a student has begun using the programs, there are many resources (easily available) to help expand his/her capabilities. All of the programs have "Help" features, Microsoft provides extensive product support and there are numerous online tutorials.

Contents

Introduction

1.1 What is a Computer

You might think of a computer as being principally for *computing*. In fact, though, computers are capable of, and are widely used for, much more than just numerical calculations. Computers are devices used for *information* processing.

The information that the computer processes can be organized in and stored as *computer "files"* and (usually) stored on some secondary storage device.

1.1.1 Computer Files

A **computer file** is a computer construct for recording and storing data in a computer storage device.

There are different types of computer files. These different types of files are designed for different purposes. A file may be designed to store a picture, a written message, a video, a computer program, or any of a wide variety of other kinds of data. Some types of files can store several types of information at once (multimedia files.)

Files are given names to allow them to be identified. A "filename" will typically have two components, the file *name* and the file *extension*. These will be written in format: "*name*" then a dot then "*extension*"

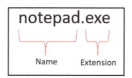

The extension normally identifies what kind of information is stored in the file.

Files with extension .exe (notepad.exe, blender.exe, …) will generally be computer programs that can be "*executed*".

Files with extension .txt (LabNotes.txt, shoppingList.txt, …) will normally be "*text*" files.

The program Microsoft Word will usually create files with extension .docx.

A file Created by the Excel program will normally have extension .xlsx.

There are a large number of extensions in common use that identify many different types of data and/or different kinds of programs that created them.

Some kinds of computer programs can open, read, change, and/or close computer files, and the computer files can be reopened, modified, and copied any number of times.

Files are organized in a *file system*, which keeps track of where the files are located on disk and lets users (and/or their programs) find and access to them.

1.1.2   File System

The file system keeps track of where on the storage device the files are stored.

Users identify the files by the *"filenames"*. The files are organized in *"directories"*

A directory is a structure that can contain files and/or other directories.

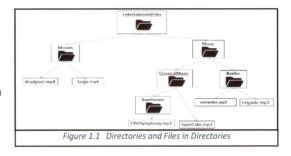

Figure 1.1   Directories and Files in Directories

(A directory contained in another directory is called a *"subdirectory"*)

Directories are also given names and users can use those names to help identify the files contained in them.

Directory names are often chosen to identify what kind of files they contain.

1.2   GUI

In order for users to *"use"* their computers, they must be provided a *"user interface"* for them to interact with. The most common kind of user interface is a *graphical user interface* (GUI).

In a graphical user interface, various elements in the computer system are represented by *icons*, (small pictures that can be displayed on the computer screen.)

These little pictures are often designed to give the user a hint as to what kind of element it represents.

The user interacts with icons using a pointing device[1], most commonly a "mouse".

1.2.1   Mouse

When the user moves the mouse on a flat surface, the mouse senses the movement and causes a "pointer" on the computer screen to make corresponding movements.

The pointer is usually a little arrow

but it can take other shapes (,   )
in certain situations.

Figure 1.2   Icons

Figure 1.2   Mouse

---

[1]   "Pointing" devices are devices that control the position of an associated "pointer" on the computer screen.

A mouse will normally have (at least) two buttons.

If the pointer is *on/over/pointing at* an icon, then the user can use the mouse buttons to interact with the icon and/or the element in the computer system element represented by that icon.

There are a number of possible interactions:

Click: If the user "clicks" with the left mouse button (presses it and the releases it) the result will usually be to "select" the icon the pointer is pointing to. This will have the effect of marking the icon or associated system element for some use in the immediate future. Clicking on an icon also has the effect of deselecting any icons that had previously been selected.

Control Click: If the user has the keyboard's control key (CTRL) depressed while clicking on an icon, then that icon will be selected and any icons previously selected will remain selected.

Shift Click: If the user has the keyboard's SHIFT key depressed while clicking on an icon, then that icon will be selected and any icons between it and previously selected icons will also be selected.

Double Click: If the user clicks twice in quick succession, the resulting action will depend on what kind of element the icon is associated with. If the icon is associated with an executable program, then double clicking on the icon will cause the computer to start executing that program. If the icon is associated with a file of a type that is usually dealt with by some specific program (a word processing program, a database manager, a browser ...[2]) then double clicking the icon will start that program running to deal with the file.

Right Click: Clicking (pressing and releasing) the right mouse button brings up a menu with additional options for whatever was clicked.

Drag: Holding down the left mouse button and moving the mouse will cause the icon to move to a new position on the screen.

Figure1.3 Right Click Menu

1.2.2 Navigating the File System

We open the file window by clicking on the File Explorer icon in the taskbar.

Figure1-4 Taskbar

---

[2]   Some file types frequently associated with specific programs include: .txt with Notepad, .docx with Microsoft Word, .xlsx with Microsoft Excel and .pptx with Microsoft PowerPoint

The file window is divided into three parts:

Ribbon[3]: Enables you to perform layout and formatting tasks

Navigation Pane: Used to access all kinds of locations: folders you've added to your favorites list, your libraries, the drives on your PC, and other PCs on your network.

Display Window: This is where the contents of the current folder or library are displayed.

1.2.2.1 Ribbon

Figure 1-7 File Window Ribbon

The ribbon display will vary depending on several factors, but the primary factors will be the elements that are active and selected in the navigation pane and the display window.

---

[3] If the ribbon fails to display, you can open it by clicking on the ˅ symbol at the right of the toolbar

Probably the most important element on the file system ribbon is the "New Folder"

icon.

There are two copies of this icon,
one located in
the upper left
corner of the
ribbon, and the

Figure 1-8 Ribbon Illustrating New Folder icons

other approximately in the ribbon's center. Clicking on either of the icons will
create a new directory.

1.2.2.1.1 New Directories

New directories must
be created in existing
directories, so in
order to use the "New
Folder" icon, you
must first have a
directory active in the
display window (for
how to activate a
directory in the
display window, see
1.2.2.2 below) to

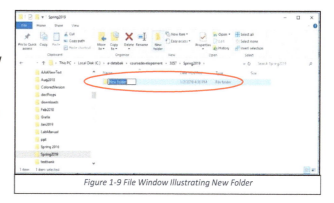

Figure 1-9 File Window Illustrating New Folder

serve as a parent directory for the new directory.

Assuming that a directory is active, simply clicking on either of the *New Folder*
icons will cause a new directory with default name "New folder" to be created in
the active directory. The directory identification field is automatically active/open
for entry, and the user can simply type the name that he/she prefers and then
press the "Enter" key.

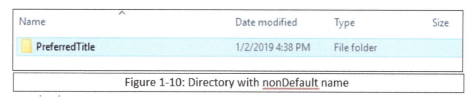

Name ⌃	Date modified	Type	Size
📁 PreferredTitle	1/2/2019 4:38 PM	File folder	

Figure 1-10: Directory with nonDefault name

1.2.2.1.2 Deleting a Directory

If you want to delete a directory (or a file) navigate to where its icon is displayed in the navigation pane and/or in the display window.

Right click on the icon (place the cursor on the icon, then press and release the right mouse button.)

A menu will open. One of the menu options is "Delete"

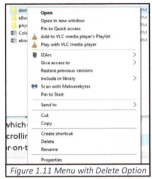

Figure 1.11 Menu with Delete Option

Click on the Delete option. You will be asked whether you want to move the file or directory to the recycle bin.

Click on "Yes" and the file or directory will be removed from the file system (to the recycle bin[4].)

Figure 1-12 Option to Send to Recycle Bin

1.2.2.2 Navigation Pane

In the Navigation pane there will be a list of directory identifiers, most of which are

marked with the folder icon

There will often be more directories than can be displayed in the navigation pane, so there will be a scrollbar on the right of the pane, and the user can change which directories are displayed by *dragging* the scrolling icon up or down (placing the cursor on the icon and then moving the cursor while holding the left mouse button down)

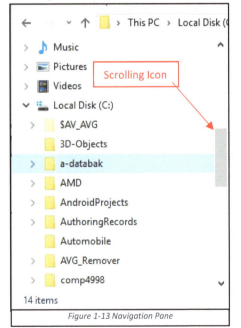

Figure 1-13 Navigation Pane

1.2.2.2.1 Directories and Subdirectories

Each directory has a name written to the right of the icon and some may have a right pointing arrow displayed to the left of the icon.

---

[4]   Items in the "recycle bin" can be returned to the file system. This gives the user a chance to later correct a deletion made by mistake. The recycle bin should be "emptied" periodically.

This arrow indicates that the directory contains other subdirectories.

Clicking on a right pointing arrow will cause the subdirectories to be displayed in the navigation pane. The subdirectories will be below the parent directory offset to its right. If a directory's subdirectories are being displayed. There will be a downward pointing arrow instead of a right pointing arrow.

If you click on a downward pointing arrow, the subdirectories will cease to be displayed and the downward pointing arrow will change to a right pointing arrow

1.2.2.2.2 Selecting a Directory

If you *select* one of the directories in the navigation pane (by clicking on it) it will be identified by a blue band in the navigation pane, and the contents of the selected directory will be displayed in the display window.

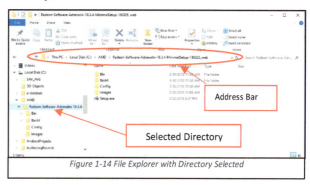

Figure 1-14 File Explorer with Directory Selected

You can also select a directory by editing the contents of the Address Bar, located just above the display window.

1.2.2.3 Display Window

The display window shows the files and subdirectories contained in the directory selected in the navigation pane

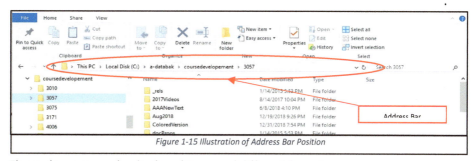

Figure 1-15 Illustration of Address Bar Position

These elements can be displayed in several different formats.

Chapter 1: Introduction

To control which display format will be used, you first click on the "View" tab in the ribbon.

Figure 1-16 Explorer Ribbon with View tab selected

Probably the most common formats are the "Details format and the Medium Icons format.

1.2.2.3.1 Details Format

With the Details format, the files and directories are displayed each grouped together, each group as a list in alphabetical order. The directories displayed first and the files next. It also displays the date of

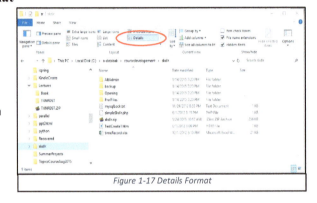

Figure 1-17 Details Format

the last modification of each, the type of element, and, in the case of the files, it indicates the sizes of the files.

1.2.2.3.2 Medium Icons Format

Using the Medium Icons format, the files and directories are represented only by (medium sized) icons representing the elements (together with their names.) Less information is

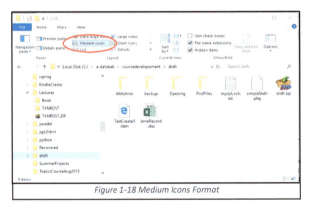

Figure 1-18 Medium Icons Format

displayed, but it is easier for a user to select the element he/she might be looking for.

1.3   Notepad

Users must have some way of creating files to be stored in the directories of their file system. One of the simplest widely available programs for doing this is *Notepad*.

Figure 1-19 Notepad Icon

Notepad is a simple text-editing program provided with the Microsoft Windows system. It enables computer users to create and edit digital documents. The files created by notepad normally have a txt extension and are pure text files. They do not have hidden formatting characters (which can be problematic for applications such as computer programs.)

Notepad will normally be used for relatively short, simple editing tasks: (shopping lists, simple computer programs, notes, ...)

Since it is so simple, it loads quickly. It does not have numerous editing options (which require extra time and attention when setting up a project and can be an extra source of confusion for a beginner.)

You open the Notepad program by clicking

on the Notepad icon[5] . An empty Notepad window will open, at which point

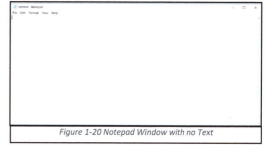
Figure 1-20 Notepad Window with no Text

you can start entering text or can open an existing file to read, print and/or edit.

1.3.1 Using Notepad to Create a New Document

As just stated, with an open notepad window you can start entering text:

1.3.1.1 Adding new text

Text entry takes effect at the position of the notepad data cursor (typically a blinking vertical line.). After some text has been entered, you can change the position of the data cursor by using the arrow keys to move it up, down, left or right. You could also simply place the mouse cursor where you want the data cursor to be and then click with the left mouse button. When the data cursor is in the position where you want tp insert new text, just start typing.

---

[5]   Found under "Windows Accessories" in the menu obtained by clicking on the ▦ icon at the lower left corner of the screen.

1.3.1.2 Deleting text

If the notepad window contains text that isn't wanted, you can delete it. Pressing the DEL key will delete the character at the right of the data cursor. Pressing the "Backspace" key delete the character at the left of the data cursor.

You can also delete text by first *selecting* a section and then pressing a key. The selected section will be deleted and, if the key pressed was that for a character to be displayed, the selected section will be replaced by that character

1.3.1.3 Selecting by dragging

You can select a section of text by placing the mouse cursor at the beginning of the desired section, pressing the left mouse button and dragging the cursor to the end of the desired section and releasing the mouse button. The selected portion will be displayed with darkened background (Figure 1-21)

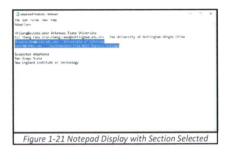

Figure 1-21 Notepad Display with Section Selected

1.3.1.4 Selecting by "Shift Click"

You can also select a section by placing the data cursor at the beginning of the desired section, then moving the mouse cursor at the end of the desired section, press the shift key and clicking with the left mouse button.

1.3.1.5 Editing: Copying, Cutting and Pasting

When a section of text has been selected, you can click on the Edit tab to display a menu and select any of several options(Figure 1-22)

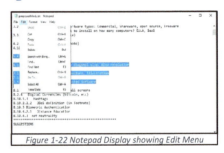

Figure 1-22 Notepad Display showing Edit Menu

(The actions available from the edit menu are also available using "short cut" key combinations without bothering to open the Edit menu)

Copy: will *copy* the selected contents to the *Clipboard*[6].
CTRL-C (hold the CTRL key down and press the C key)

---

[6]   The *clipboard* is a section of memory where data can be stored in order to later transfer (copies of) that data to other locations in a notepad file. It can also be used to copy that data into other notepad files or other applications (Word documents, Excel files, etc.)

Cut: will *cut* the selected section out of the document, i.e. copy the selected contents into the Clipboard and delete the selected section from the document.
CTRL-X (hold the CTRL key down and press the X key)

Paste: will copy the contents of the clipboard into the document If a section of text is selected, the contents of the clipboard will replace the text in the selected section. If no text is selected, the clipboard contents will be inserted into the document at the location of the data cursor.
CTRL-V (hold the CTRL key down and press the V key)

1.3.1.6 Editing: Searching and Replacing

When working with a large document, you will often want to find a place where a particular word or phrase occurs.

The Editing menu provides two tools to support this type of operation.

Find: Will search (either downward or upward) through the document to find an occurrence of text chosen by user and place the data cursor where it is found. The user must, of course, see to it that the text being sought is in the text box in the dialog box that appears.
CTRL-F (hold the CTRL key down and press the F key)
(See Figure 1-23)

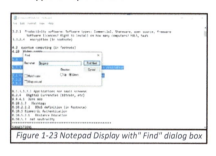
Figure 1-23 Notepad Display with" Find" dialog box

Replace: Will search (either downward or upward) through the document to find an occurrence of text chosen by user, will place the data cursor at that location and will replace that text with different text. The user must, of course, see to it that the proper text strings are entered in each of the text boxes in the dialog box that appears.
CTRL-H (hold the CTRL key down and press the H key)
(See Figure 1-24)

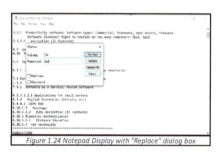
Figure 1.24 Notepad Display with "Replace" dialog box

1.3.1.7 Saving a Notepad Document as a File

When a document has been edited into the form that you want it, then it should probably be saved to disk for some future use.

Notepad offers two options for saving a document. If you click on the "File" tab, a menu will appear showing options (Figure 1-25):

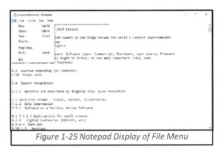

Figure 1-25 Notepad Display of File Menu

"Save" Which will save the document, in its current form, with the current name, replacing the version of the document with that name currently on the disk. Use of

this option assumes that the current document has been assigned a name and is associated with an earlier version of the document which is stored on disk. The same thing is accomplished by pressing CTRL-S while in normal document display.

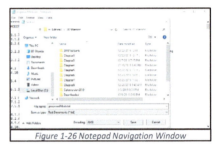

Figure 1-26 Notepad Navigation Window

"Save as" Which will open a navigation window. You can use this window to select a directory where the file will be stored, and then you can enter a file name for the document. (Figure 1-26)

1.3.2 Using Notepad to Open an Existing File

To open an existing file from the notepad window, you click on the File tab and select "Open" from the menu that appears(Figure 1-27) This opens a dialog box similar to the file window, with a navigation panel and display window (as in Figure 1-28)

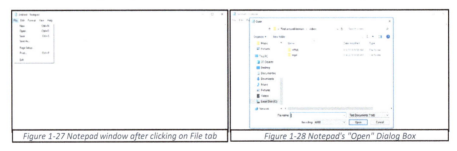

| *Figure 1-27 Notepad window after clicking on File tab* | *Figure 1-28 Notepad's "Open" Dialog Box* |

You can use the navigation panel to navigate and select directories (the path to the selected directory will be displayed in the address bar.) By default, the display window shows directories and .txt files in the selected directory (Figure 1-29 below.)

The types of files that will be displayed can be changed by changing the setting in the document display type box. The alternative setting is *.* which will result in *all* files in the selected directory to be displayed (as in Figure 1-30.)

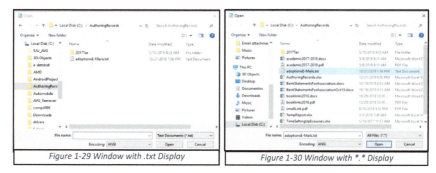

| Figure 1-29 Window with .txt Display | Figure 1-30 Window with *.* Display |

If one of files is selected, then its name will be displayed in the "File name" box beneath the display window.

When you have selected a file, you can click on the "Open" box/button. The selected file will open in the Notepad window and you can view and edit the contents of the Notepad document.

1.3.3 Opening a Notepad Document from the File System Window

You can also open notepad documents directly from the file system window.

Figure 1-31 File Open in Notepad

You double click on an icon representing a .txt file. In this case a Notepad window will open and the content of the file will display in the window.

Figure 1-32 File Directory with .txt

You might also right click on a file icon (not necessarily a .txt file.) The menu will open. You would select "Open with" from the menu and, from its submenu find and click on "Notepad" (See Figure 1-33) A Notepad window would open and the content of the selected file would display.

Figure 1-33 Illustration of "Open

1.3.4 Printing a Notepad Document

The File menu also includes an entry for printing the document. If you click on this entry, the print dialog window will open.

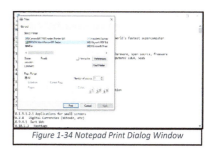

This window allows you to select the printer to be used, as well as the number of copies to print and other printing factors.

Pressing CTRL-P while in document display will print the document directly on the default printer.

Figure 1-34 Notepad Print Dialog Window

1.3.5 Closing a Document

When you have finished working on a document (and have saved any information you will want to reference later and have done any printing you want to have done) you should close the document window.

There are two ways you could do this.

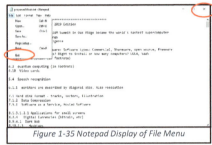

1. Open the menu under the File tab and click on "Exit"
2. Click on the x in the upper right corner of the window. (This will close most windows in Microsoft Windows system).

Figure 1-35 Notepad Display of File Menu

1.3.6 Notepad Help

Like most Microsoft applications, the Notepad window includes a "Help" tab

Since Notepad was designed to be simple and use very few resources, the application itself does not include any actual help information. The "View Help" option is a link to online resources. These resources are, of course, quite extensive, but they do require Internet access.

1.4 Accessing the Internet

One of the main uses of computers today is to access the Internet, and most commonly the World Wide Web. You access the World Wide Web using a program called a *browser*. There are a number of different browsers, but most of them share common features.

The browser we will discuss here is called Microsoft *Edge*.

1.4.1 Internet Addresses

The Internet consists of a large number of computers and communications devices, all of which are interconnected in a huge communications network.

Each site in this network is identified by an IP address (a combination of four numbers separated by dots or periods e.g. 72.21.211.176) Many of the sites (the ones we are generally most interested in) are also assigned a text identification called a *uniform resource locater* (more commonly referred to as a URL. Also sometimes referred to as a uniform resource i*dentifier* or URI.)

A typical URL could have the form   *(protocol)://(hostname)/(filename)*

Example: http://www.example.com/index.html ,

       this illustrates a *protocol* (http), a *hostname* (www.example.com), and a *file name* (index.html)

It is common to specify URL's without identifying a protocol (in which case the default protocol http or https will be used) and/or without specifying a filename (in which case a default file name will be used, often index.html)

Examples of URL's:

https://mail.google.com/mail/u/1/#inbox
http://correo.upr.edu/
ftp://ftp.gnu.org/

1.4.2 Opening the Browser

When you want to access the World Wide Web, you would start by executing a program called a *browser*. You click on the appropriate icon ![e], a window will open with displaying the Web page from a default URL. (See Figure 1-36)

Figure 1.36 Edge Browser with display from www.google.com

You *can* get a new Web page, change the display in the browser window by entering a URL in the address bar. (Figure 1-37 shows, most browsers will show suggested URL values as we type.)

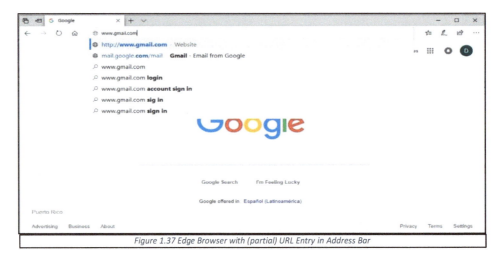

Figure 1.37 Edge Browser with (partial) URL Entry in Address Bar

It is much more common, however, to open a display in the browser window by clicking on a link in the browser display window. A *link* (more precisely a *hyperlink*) is a object (a section of text, or an image) that is associated with another Web item (most commonly a Web page.) When you click with the cursor pointing to a *link,* the browser will attempt to retrieve and display the item associated with that link.

You can tell if the cursor points to a link because then it will have the form of a finger. If the cursor is pointing to a link (which can be a section of text, as in figure 1-38 or it can be an image.)

Figure 1-38 Edge Browser with Cursor pointing to Link

1.5   E-Mail

Email is a system for exchanging messages by means of the Internet and is one of the oldest services provided by the Internet.

Today's email systems are based on a "store-and-forward" model. That means, when a user sends an email message, it gets "stored" in an account on an email "server" and remains there until the intended recipient logs into that account and downloads the message. The sending user and the destination user do not have to be online at the same time. Each needs to be online only for as long as it takes to send or receive the message.

There are many email servers. Some of the better known are yahoo, hotmail and gmail. Most companies of any size have e-mail servers for their employees to use. Schools often have e-mail servers for their faculty and students.

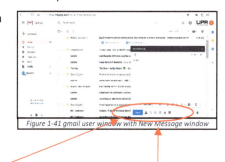

Figure 1-39 gmail user window

To access your email messages, you enter the url of the server (see figure 1-37 above), then identify the email account

(john.smith28@gmail.com, juan.garcia12@upr.edu, …), You enter the password for the account and the user window will open, displaying messages that the account has received. Clicking on one of the entries will open that message and display it in the email window.

Figure 1-40 gmail user window with open message

The first email systems could only handle text messages, but now emails can contain multimedia (images, sound and videos) as well.

You can also use the email system to send your own emails. In order to send an email from the gmail system, you begin by clicking on the "+ Compose" symbol in upper left part of the gmail window. A "New Message" window will open.

Figure 1-41 gmail user window with New Message window

You can type text directly into the New Message window or you can copy text or graphics from the clipboard into the New Message window.

You can also use the New Message control bar

to insert photos into the message

to insert contents of a file from the cloud

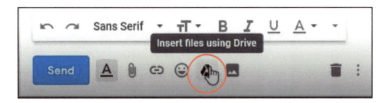

to insert an emoji

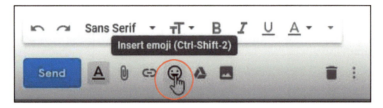

to insert a hyperlink

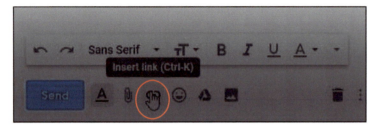

to attach a file to be sent along with the message

1.6 E-Mail Example:

In this example, we will illustrate how you might use email to send a recipe to a friend.

1.6.1 The recipe ingredient list in Notepad

The list of ingredients for the recipe is a little long Figure 1-42.) It will be better to compose the list "offline" using a program designed for text editing (Notepad for example) and then copy it into the New Message window. Using a text editing program, it will be easier to correct errors, make substitutions, modifications, etc.

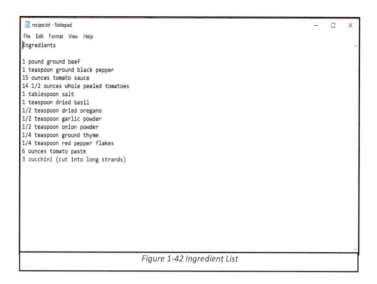

Figure 1-42 Ingredient List

1.6.2 Starting the Email

Open the "compose message" email application, enter the email address of the intended recipient and enter a brief message for him/her.

Figure 1-43 Initial Email Composition

1.6.3 Inserting the Ingredient List

Copy the list of ingredients into the clipboard (select, then CTRL-C) and paste it (with CTRL-V) into the composition window.

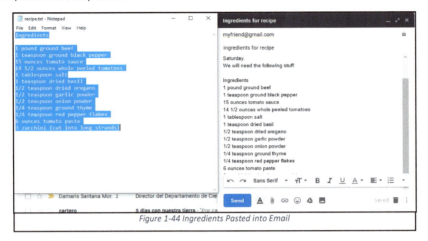

Figure 1-44 Ingredients Pasted into Email

1.6.4 Attaching Picture

You might also want to "attach" a picture of the dish. Click on the "Attach file" icon and, when the selection window opens, navigate to the directory with the image, select the file with the picture of the ZucchiniSpaghetti and click the "Open} button

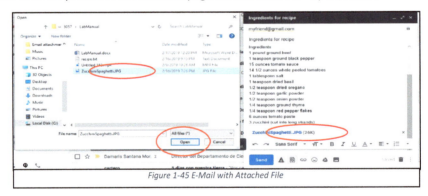

Figure 1-45 E-Mail with Attached File

1.7 Exercises:

1.7.1 Exercise 1

Create and send an email with a list of at least 5 names and phone numbers

1.7.2 Exercise 2

Create and send an email with a photo of yourself attached

1.7.3 Exercise 3

Create and send an email with a recipe. The body of the email should include a list of ingredients (as in example 1.6) A text file with the preparation instructions should be attached to the email.)

Word Processing

2.1 Introduction to Microsoft Word

As mentioned earlier, Notepad is a good program to use for the creation of short simple documents with only text and no complex formatting. For bigger projects a more complex program is needed. One of the most widely used word processing programs is Microsoft Word.

To open the Word program, you simply click on the Word icon and a Word window will open. (Figure 2-1.)

Figure 2-1 Initial Word Window

The initial display includes:

several icons identifying some standard document templates that can be used when creating a new document 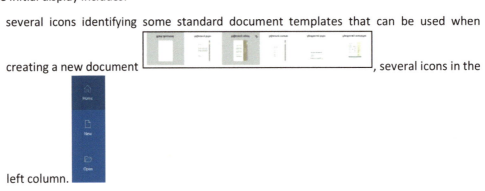, several icons in the left column.

and a list of recently edited documents

If you click on one of the entries in the list of recently edited documents, that document will be opened for further editing.

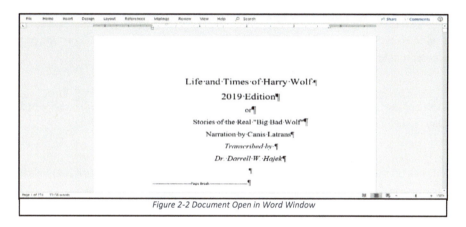

Figure 2-2 Document Open in Word Window

One of the left column icons New is for creating a new document (using one of several predefined templates) and another of the left column icons Open is be used for searching for an existing document.

If you click on the left column "Open" icon Open a new window will open with support for navigation for locating existing documents for you to open.

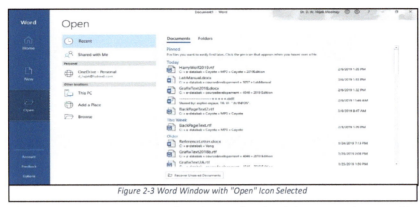

Figure 2-3 Word Window with "Open" Icon Selected

This window provides a more extensive list of recently edited documents (arranged in order of access, most recent first.)

The left column also has a "home" icon [Home icon] If you click this icon, the original word window display (see Figure 2-1) will return.

If you click on the left column [New icon] icon, the "New" window opens (Figure 2-4) This window displays several different styles for Word documents that you might use.

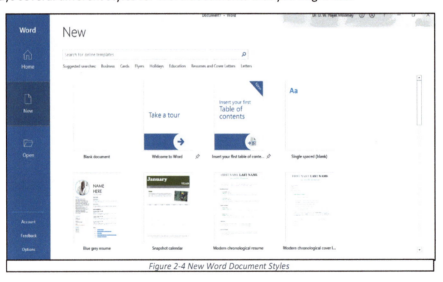

Figure 2-4 New Word Document Styles

2.2 Word Example 1: Job Application

In order to start your example document, you can open the Microsoft Word program [W icon], as

described above, select the New option [New icon], to arrive at display as in Figure 2-4, above.

Click on the "Blank Document" [icon] icon. The blank editing screen will open (Figure 2-5).

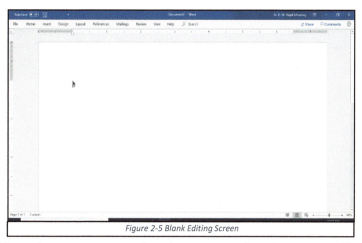

Figure 2-5 Blank Editing Screen

It will probably not be necessary very often, but you can adjust the page size (the height and width of the paper that the document would be printed on) and the widths of the margins. These controls can be found in the ribbon that opens if you click on the "Layout" tab

In the initial (blank) editing screen you will probably see the ¶ symbol with a blinking vertical

line beside it. There will probably be a mouse cursor somewhere on the screen as well. The ¶ symbol is a "*paragraph marker*" a *non-printing* character (more about non-printing characters shortly) and the blinking line is the *insertion pointer*. The insertion pointer marks the position where our data entry will take effect.

As you type, the letters will appear on the screen at the place marked by the insertion pointer

Chapter 2: Microsoft Word

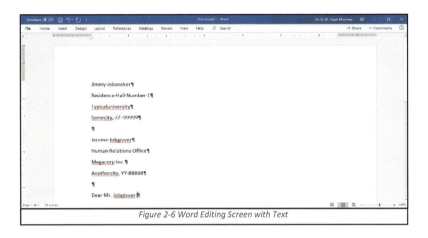

Figure 2-6 Word Editing Screen with Text

2.2.1 Non-Printing Characters

You will notice in the example in Figure 2-6 that each line ends with the symbol¶ and that the different words are separated by a dot. These are non printing characters (formatting markers).

Non-printing characters, or **formatting marks**, are characters identifying content *design* in word processors. They aren't displayed at printing. They control the *format* (the way that text is displayed or printed) but do not result in any output themselves. The most common of the formatting marks are:

¶   paragraph break

.   single space

→   tab

↵   line break

Many people do not like to have the formatting characters displayed while they are editing, preferring to see their text "the way it would look".

You can suppress the display of the formatting characters. First click on the "Home" ribbon tab to display its associated ribbon.

Figure 2-7 Home Tab Ribbon

One of the buttons in the "Home" ribbon is the "Show/Hide" button ¶ .

When the button has a shaded background (as shown above) the non printing characters will be displayed. If you click on the ¶ button, its background will change to white ¶ and the non printing characters in the document body will not be displayed.

If you click on the white background button, its background will change back to shaded and the non printing characters in the document body will reappear

26

2.2.2 Paragraph Alignment

You will note that, in our example, the first four lines, identifying the name and address of the person sending the letter, are all positioned at the left of the page. Names and addresses of this kind are more traditionally located in the center of the page.

In order to position this text in the center of the page, first *select* the text to be repositioned (place the mouse pointer at the beginning of the text and left click, then place the pointer at the end of the text, hold the shift key down and left click. The desired text should be highlighted. Figure 2-8)

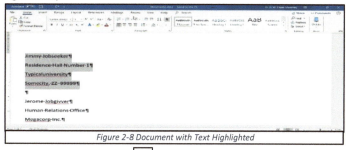

Figure 2-8 Document with Text Highlighted

Next find the "Center Content" icon ▤ in the Home ribbon. When you click on this icon, its background will change to a darker shade, ▤ and the selected text will move to center of the page (Figure 2-9).

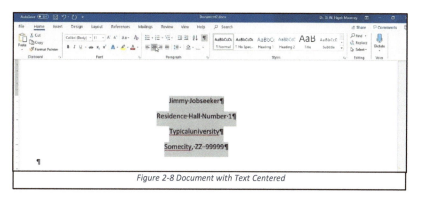

Figure 2-8 Document with Text Centered

2.2.3 Line Separation

The different lines of the name and address section that we have just centered look a little far apart. Technically, they are not different *lines*, they are different *paragraphs*, since they are separated by the paragraph separator ¶. We can improve the appearance by replacing the paragraph separators with line separators ↵

One at a time, place the pointer at a paragraph separator and click, to locate the data cursor at that point. Press the DEL key to erase the paragraph separator, then press the Shift key and the Enter key (the Shift-Enter combination results in a "*soft* line break")

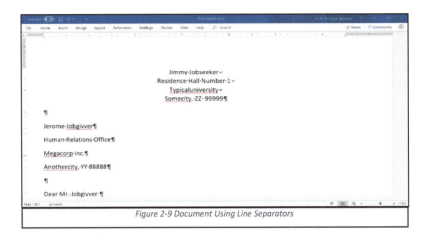

Figure 2-9 Document Using Line Separators

Of course the addressee field (i.e. the address where the letter is to be sent) should probably have the same line separation format.

2.2.4 Font Face and Font Size

It is common to display the "return address" at the top of a letter with a different appearance than the text in the rest of the document.

To change the "font face" of a section of text you select that section and then, in the Home ribbon, click on the down arrow beside the font name and, in the menu that appears, we you scroll down to the appearance we prefer and select that font (Figure 2-10)

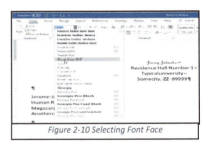

Figure 2-10 Selecting Font Face

In the font section of the Home ribbon you can also adjust the *size* of the text 18 ⌄ as well as the font style, (i.e. whether **Bold** B *Italicized* I Underlined U etc.) and color of the text. A

2.2.5 Date

It is customary to include the date of a letter.

In the *Insert* ribbon there is an icon that will insert the current date into a document.

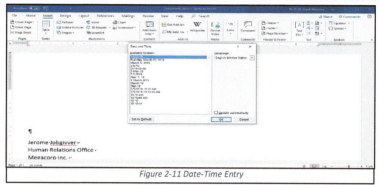

Figure 2-11 Date-Time Entry

As you can see in Figure 2-11, there are a lot of options for the format that can be used for displaying dates and times.

The date at the top of a letter is normally positioned at the right side of the page (right justified) and this can be accomplished in the paragraph section of the Home ribbon .

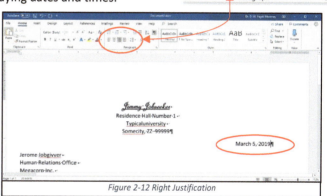

Figure 2-12 Right Justification

2.2.6 Saving the Document

When you have finished the document (or simply want to stop, and continue editing later) you can save it to secondary storage.

If you are working on a document that had been saved before, then you can save the updated version by simply clicking on the "Save" icon in the upper left corner of the screen[7].

If you have not saved the document before, you will initiate the "saving new document" process by clicking on the *File* tab and then selecting the *"Save As"* option from the list of options in the left column of the page that appears (Figure 2-13)

---

[7]   It is recommended that this be done at regular intervals if you are doing extensive editing. It can be very frustrating if the computer suddenly stops working and you lose the results of a lot of work.

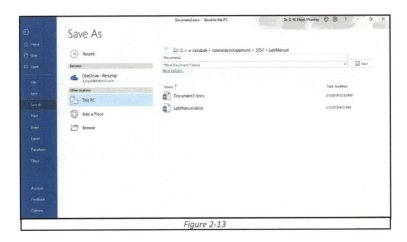

Figure 2-13

From the "Save As" page you can assign a name to the document by entering the desired name in the name block (as in Figure 2-14)

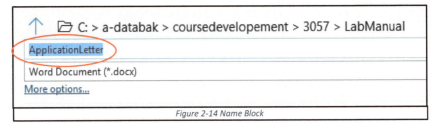

Figure 2-14 Name Block

From the "Save As" page you can also choose a directory where the document will be stored.

To choose a directory, you click on *directory* line (just above the name block) and, in the resulting popup window (Figure 2-15), you navigate to the directory you want.

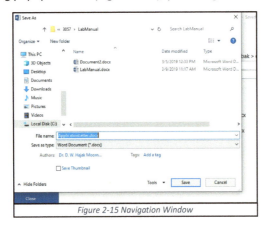

Figure 2-15 Navigation Window

Another thing you can do from the "Save As" page is to modify the format to be used for the document file.

If you click on the down arrow at the right end of the document format box, a window will open displaying many options (Figure 2-16).

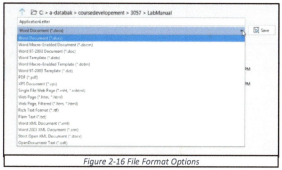

Figure 2-16 File Format Options

2.2.6.1 Document File Formats

Although Microsoft Word supports many different file formats, four of these formats are especially widely used.

.docx This is the default format for Microsoft Word and should probably the format used unless there is some reason to choose another format. In particular, the docx format should be preferred if the document will be reviewed and/or re-edited using Microsoft Word. If, however, a document is stored in docx format, viewing it or editing it using another program can be problematic.

.pdf This is a file format developed by Adobe in the 1990s to present documents, including text formatting and images, in a manner independent of application software, hardware, and operating systems. A document stored in pdf format will generally require less storage space than a docx document producing similar appearance. This format was designed to reproduce the appearance of the documents, not to facilitate editing of documents.

.rtf This is a file format that will include all of the formatting controls (non-printing characters) in the document. Most word processors can read and write rtf formatted files. This format would be a good choice for a file intended to be shared with other people who might be expected to make modifications and who might not be using Microsoft Word to do so. A file in rtf format will generally be larger than a similar file in docx format.

.txt A TXT file is a standard text document that contains unformatted text. It is recognized by any text editing or word processing program and can also be processed by most other software programs. TXT files are useful for storing information in plain text with no special formatting beyond basic fonts and font styles. The file is commonly used for recording notes, directions, and other similar documents that do not need to appear a certain way.

2.2.7 Paragraph Indentation and/or Spacing

Within the body of a document, there are two traditional ways to separate paragraphs: *indentation* and *spacing*.

These are not the *only* alternatives, but they are by far the most common.

You can control these characteristics of your paragraphs (as well as several others) using the "Paragraph" dialog box. We open this dialog box by, first selecting the text in the paragraph whose characteristics you want to set, and then clicking on the little arrow at the bottom right corner of the "Paragraph" section in the "Home" ribbon.

The Paragraph dialog box will open to display several boxes which provide controls for characteristics of the selected paragraphs.

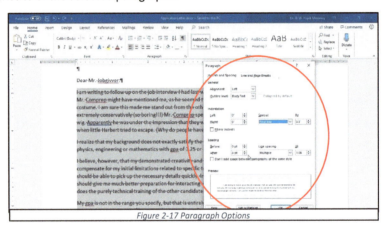

Figure 2-17 Paragraph Options

2.2.7.1 Paragraph Spacing

The "Spacing" control boxes allow you to require each affected paragraph have blank space above and/or below. How much space should be used will depend on the size of the text in the paragraphs, larger text requiring more space to signal the beginning of a new paragraph. As a general rule, 6 pt or 8 pt[8] is a reasonable size.

---

[8] "point" is a measure traditionally used to describe font sizes. One point is approximately 1/72 inch.

2.2.7.2 First Line indentation

As an alternative to putting extra space between paragraphs, you might choose to

indent the first line of each paragraph. The "Special" box allows you to do that.

First line indentation was commonly used when manual typewriters were common, and fine control of the vertical positioning of text was relatively difficult. It is not so common now. Combining paragraph spacing and first line indentation is considered overkill (one of the many things that our fictional Jimmy Jobseeker does not seem to understand.)

2.2.8 Spelling Checking and Grammar Checking

In the body of the example letter, an observant reader will notice a few words with red or blue underlines. These mark words or phrases that might be misspellings or grammatical errors.

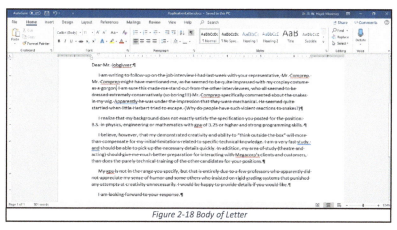

Figure 2-18 Body of Letter

The red underlining marks words that the Microsoft Word system has identified as possibly spelling errors. Word marks each document word that it does not find in it's dictionary. In this example letter, most the words marked in red are proper names, which, of course, would not be found in a dictionary. It also marked "gpa" which will not be found in most dictionaries either but is certainly a term that Mr. Jobseeker wanted to use. The user should treat these markings as suggestions, not as commands.

Blue underlines mark (probable) grammatical errors. In the example letter the blue lines identify possible errors in use of commas. Again, blue lines should be treated as suggestions, not as commands.

2.2.9 Exercises

2.2.9.1 Write a letter that Mr. Jobgivver might send to Mr. Jobseeker in response to his application. Save the letter/document as a .docx file. Create an email with the letter as an attachment.

2.2.9.2 Write a letter addressed to an academic administrator protesting a grade. Save the letter/document as a .docx file. Create an email with the letter as an attachment.

2.2.9.3 Write a letter addressed to a credit card company requesting a charge that appeared on your statement be cancelled. Save the letter/document as a .docx file. Create an email with the letter as an attachment.

2.3 Word Example 2: Second Letter

If a document has been saved, it can be re-opened later for re-editing.

In our example, if Mr. Jobseeker receives no response to his application (previous section) he might decide to send a followup, and, having a copy of his earlier letter with names and addresses already in place, he might start his followup letter by editing a copy of the earlier letter, rather than entering everything again.

He can open the existing document by first clicking on the folder icon 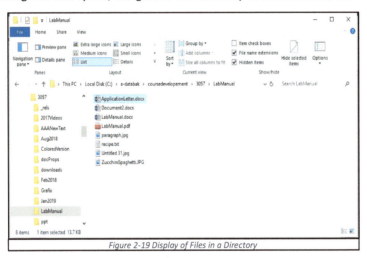 in the taskbar and, in the dialog box that opens, navigate to the directory with the desired file.

Figure 2-19 Display of Files in a Directory

If you double click on a docx file, Microsoft Word will open the file for editing.

You could also *right* click on the entry for the file. Right click opens a menu of options, one of which is "Open". Clicking on "Open" in the menu will open the file using the default application for the file type ("Microsoft Word" for a docx file)

"Open with" is yet another option in the right click menu. "Open with" provides a submenu from which you can select an application other than a default application associated with a file type.

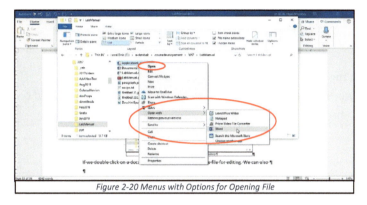

Figure 2-20 Menus with Options for Opening File

2.3.1 Adding an Image

A Word document can include images as well as text. In our example, Mr. Jobseeker might decide that his letters should have a logo in the letterhead. With the data entry cursor at the top of the letter, he could click on the "Insert" tab to display the Insert ribbon.

When he clicks on the "Pictures" icon in the "Insert" ribbon,

 a navigation window will open, and he can navigate to the directory with the desired image[9] (see Figure 2-21)

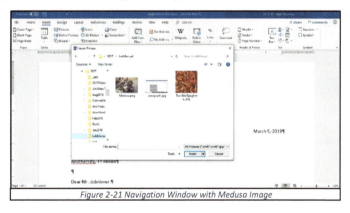

Figure 2-21 Navigation Window with Medusa Image

---

[9]   Remember that Jimmy has a thing for snakes.

He would select the appropriate image and click on the "Insert" button
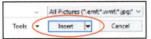 at the bottom of the window. This will insert the selected

image at the data insertion point

This, however, is not where he would want the logo to be positioned on the page. In order

to reposition the image, he might right click the image to open a menu

Placing the cursor on ("hovering" over) the "Wrap Text" icon opens
a submenu and, from that submenu he could select the "In Front of Text" option.

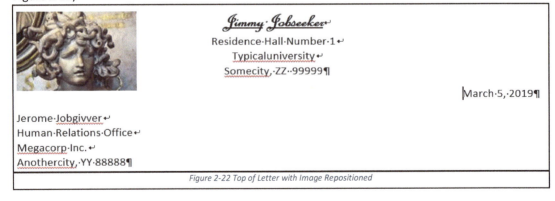

With that option selected, the image can be "dragged" to a more appropriate location (as in Figure 2-22)

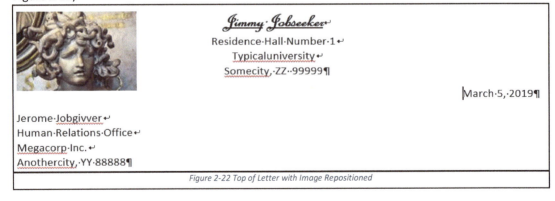

Figure 2-22 Top of Letter with Image Repositioned

2.3.2 Bulleted Paragraphs

Mr. Jobseeker might decide to make his arguments more effectively if he presents them in the form of a "bulleted" list.

To change the formatting of active (i.e. selected) paragraphs to "Bulleted List" he would click on the "Bullet" icon  in the Paragraph section of the Home ribbon.

This would convert the paragraph formatting to that of "Bullets".

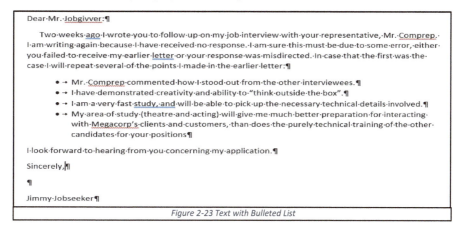

Dear·Mr.·Jobgivver:¶

    Two·weeks·ago·I·wrote·you·to·follow·up·on·my·job·interview·with·your·representative,·Mr.·Comprep.· I·am·writing·again·because·I·have·received·no·response.·I·am·sure·this·must·be·due·to·some·error,·either· you·failed·to·receive·my·earlier·letter·or·your·response·was·misdirected.·In·case·that·the·first·was·the· case·I·will·repeat·several·of·the·points·I·made·in·the·earlier·letter:¶

    •→ Mr.·Comprep·commented·how·I·stood·out·from·the·other·interviewees.¶
    •→ I·have·demonstrated·creativity·and·ability·to·"think·outside·the·box".¶
    •→ I·am·a·very·fast·study,·and·will·be·able·to·pick·up·the·necessary·technical·details·involved.¶
    •→ My·area·of·study·(theatre·and·acting)·will·give·me·much·better·preparation·for·interacting· with·Megacorp's·clients·and·customers,·than·does·the·purely·technical·training·of·the·other· candidates·for·your·positions¶

I·look·forward·to·hearing·from·you·concerning·my·application.¶

Sincerely,¶

¶

Jimmy·Jobseeker¶

Figure 2-23 Text with Bulleted List

2.3.3 Fully Justified Paragraphs

Notice that the right ends of the lines in the main paragraph in the letter are not aligned.

If Mr. Jobseeker were to decide that he prefers the paragraph be fully justified (all lines, except possibly the first, begin in the same column and all lines, with the exception of the last) end in the same column, he would first set the data entry cursor in the paragraph in question, and then click on the "Justify" icon in the Paragraph section of the Home ribbon.

Doing this would *Justify* the selected paragraph.

Two·weeks·ago·I·wrote·you·to·follow·up·on·my·job·interview·with·your·representative,·Mr.·Comprep.· I·am·writing·again·because·I·have·received·no·response.·I·am·sure·this·must·be·due·to·some·error,·either· you·failed·to·receive·my·earlier·letter·or·your·response·was·misdirected.·In·case·that·the·first·was·the·case· I·will·repeat·several·of·the·points·I·made·in·the·earlier·letter:¶

2.3.4 Help Features in Word

The Microsoft Word tabs include two help features, the "Search" tab and the "Help" tab.

You can also get help by pressing the F1 key.

2.3.4.1 The Search Tab

If you click on the "Search" tab  a small window will open  with a line in which you can enter a description of what you want information/help about. As you type your entry, below the line will be a number of suggestions that will change while you type, as the system keeps

trying to "guess" what it is you are entering.

The "Search" function will search through the active document, through the functions/operations available and through the Internet.

2.3.4.2 The Help Tab

If you click on the "Help" tab, the "Help" ribbon will display several options

Clicking on the Help icon 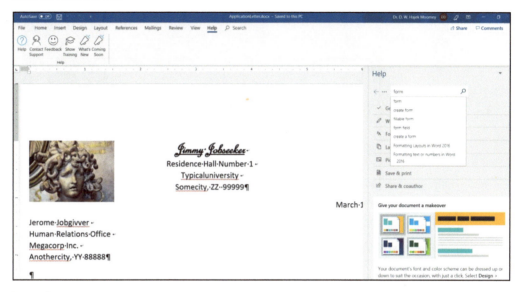 in the help ribbon will open the "Help column" on the right of the screen where you can enter whatever it is you want information about.

2.3.5 Exercises

2.3.5.1 Write a letter that Mr. Jobgivver might send to Mr. Jobseeker in response to the letter of this section. Include a company logo and bullet list responding to each of Jobseeker's bulleted points. Save the letter in a file. Save the letter/document as a .docx file. Create an email with the letter as an attachment.

2.3.5.2 Write a letter addressed to a professor protesting a grade. Add a "School Logo" Include a list of reasons why the grade should be better. Save the letter/document as a .docx file. Create an email with the letter as an attachment.

2.3.5.3 Write a letter that a tourist agency might send a potential customer explaining why he/she/they should book a vacation with their agency. Save the letter/document as a .docx file. Create an email with the letter as an attachment.

Spreadsheets

An *electronic spreadsheet* is a program that allows the user to manipulate information in cells laid out in a rectangular table. A cell can typically contain a number, some text or a formula for computing values to be displayed in the cell. Spreadsheet users can adjust any stored value and observe the effects on calculated values. This makes the spreadsheet useful for "what-if" analysis since many cases can be rapidly investigated without manual recalculation.

The word 'spreadsheet' came from 'spread' as with a newspaper or magazine that opens (spreads) into two facing pages, with information extending across the center fold and treating the two pages as one large page.

The compound word 'spread-sheet' came to be used to describe the format used in book-keeping ledgers—with columns for categories of expenditures across the top, invoices listed down the left margin, and the amount of each payment in the cell where its row and column intersect. The ledgers traditionally used many columns which required two facing pages, or oversized sheets of paper (termed 'analysis paper') ruled into rows and columns, approximately twice as wide as ordinary paper.

3.1 Opening a Project with Microsoft Excel

Microsoft Excel is the spreadsheet program in the Microsoft Office suite.

In this project we will illustrate the construction of a spreadsheet which a professor might develop to track progress of students in a class, and, at the end of the course, compute the grades for the students.

To create the Microsoft Excel spreadsheet, we can begin by finding and clicking on the *"Excel"* icon to open the Excel Home window.

Figure 3-1 Excel Home Window

3.1.1 Creating the New Spreadsheet

Since the project is the creation of a "New" spreadsheet, we should click on the "New" icon in the left column.

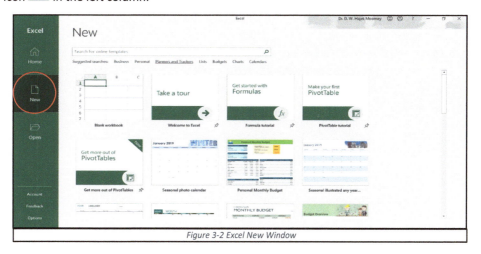

Figure 3-2 Excel New Window

The "New" window displays a number of options for opening preformatted sheets for calendars, budgets, tutorials, schedules, reports and others.

For this project we would select the "Blank workbook" option 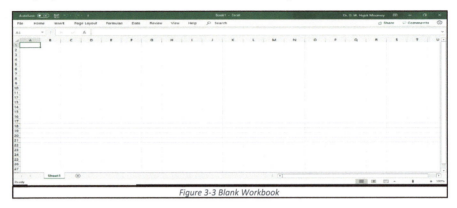.[10]

Figure 3-3 Blank Workbook

The columns in an Excel spreadsheet are identified by letters (and, for columns further to the right, multiple letters.) The rows of the spreadsheet are identified by numbers. Each cell is located in a column and in a row, and so, can be identified using a pair, a letter (or pair of letters) identifying the column, and a number identifying the row.

3.1.2 Structuring the Spreadsheet for the Class: *Identifiers*

Let us assume that, in the class the spreadsheet describes, the professor plans to give 5 quizzes and 4 examinations. The data of each type will be stored in its own column, so we would begin designing the sheet by entering identifiers at the top of each column: Name, Quiz1, Quiz2, Quiz3, Quiz4, Quiz5, Exam1, Exam2, Exam3 and Exam4.

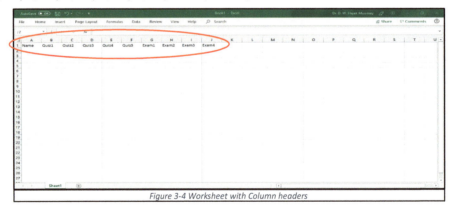

Figure 3-4 Worksheet with Column headers

---

[10]   (Alternatively, you could have simply immediately clicked on the "Blank Workbook" icon ⬜ in the top row of the "Home" window instead of the "New" icon and *then* the "Blank Workbook" icon.)

The student names will be entered in the left column

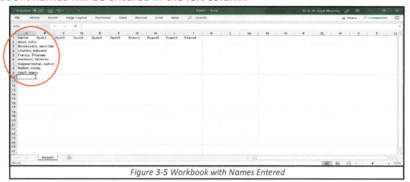

Figure 3-5 Workbook with Names Entered

You will notice that the names do not fit in the default space occupied by the column. We want to make the column space wider. We place the cursor in the column heading row at the division between column A and column B markers. The cursor changes to a double

arrow.

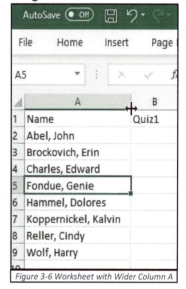

Figure 3-6 Worksheet with Wider Column A

Press the left mouse button and drag cursor to the right until the column is wide enough that all of the names fit comfortably in the space provided. (See Figure 3-6)

3.1.3 Structuring the Spreadsheet for the Class: Inserting a Row

Suppose another student, Paloma Delasilla, enrolls in the class at this point. If we want the roster to continue to display the records in alphabetical order, her grades (and name) should come between those of "Charles, Edward" and "Fondue, Genie".

To insert a blank row for Delasilla's records, we would begin by selecting a cell in Fondue's row (as shown in Figure 3-6.)

In the "Home" ribbon, we click under the "Insert" icon,

and, in the dropdown menu that results, select "Insert Sheet Rows"

This will insert a blank row into the worksheet above the row with the selected cell

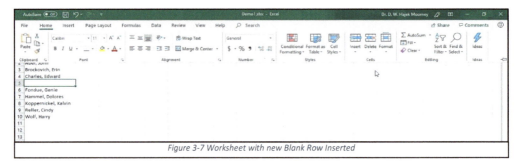

Figure 3-7 Worksheet with new Blank Row Inserted

and now we can enter Paloma's name in the worksheet where it belongs.

3.1.4 Structuring the Spreadsheet for the Class: Inserting a Column

When the professor in charge of this class comes to assign grades, he will probably be more interested in the *average* quiz scores and average exam scores for each of the students, rather than the individual scores themselves.

It would be natural to list the averages at the ends of the lists of quiz and exam scores. But to do that, there must be spaces to store the averages, so we must insert a new column with spaces for the quiz averages. First, we select a cell in the column to the right of where we want the new column (select a cell in column G, the "Exam 1" column.)

Then in the "Home" ribbon, click the arrow under the "Insert" icon (just as like we did when with inserting a row) but this time we click on "Insert Sheet *Columns*"

This inserts a new column to the left of "Exam 1" and moves all of the "Exam" columns one space to the right.

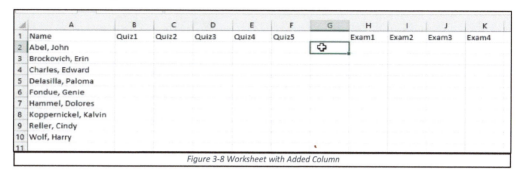

Figure 3-8 Worksheet with Added Column

We should now put a label ("Average") at the top of this column

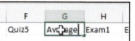

to identify what kind of data will be displayed in the cells below.

3.1.5 Structuring the Spreadsheet for the Class: Inserting a Function

Of course, putting the label at the top of the column does nothing to insert averages in the cells in the column below that label.

In order to make the spreadsheet calculate the quiz score averages, we begin by selecting

cell G2 (the cell immediately below the one where we put the label "Average".)

We then click on the little arrow at the right of the "Autosum" icon in the "Editing" group

of the "Home" Ribbon and, when the dropdown menu appears, we select

"Average"

This inserts the "AVERAGE function into cell G2

(Note that "=AVERAGE()" also appears in the formula bar above the worksheet.)

This has identified the *function* to be calculated, but we have not yet identified the values to calculate the average of.

We place the cursor over the B2 cell, press the left mouse button, drag the cursor over to the F2 cell and release the mouse button.

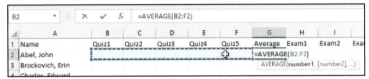

The "B2:F2" entry indicates that the function is to calculate the average of all numbers found in the cells between the B2 cell and the F2 cell. These are exactly the values the professor will want the averages of (at least in the case of John Abel.)

Since the function has been set up correctly, we click "Enter" (the check mark in the box

to the left of the function bar.)

The **#DIV/0!** display in the G2 cell is a *"division by zero"* error identification.

The AVERAGE function calculates the sum of the numbers to be averaged and divides by the number of nonempty entries.

In this case, there are no quiz grades (as yet) so calculating the average would involve division by zero. The error message will be replaced by a number, once the professor enters a few numbers into cells between B2 and F2.

3.1.6 Structuring the Spreadsheet for the Class: Copying Functions

The formula, at this point, only calculates the average for one student, John Abel. The professor will want the averages for all of the students. We will copy the function into all of the cells of column G.

Place the cursor on the little dot at the bottom right corner of the G2 cell.

The cursor changes form to a small + symbol.

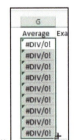

Press the left mouse button and drag the cursor down to the G10 cell and release the mouse button. Click on any cell outside the G2 through G10 range to *accept* the copied functions.

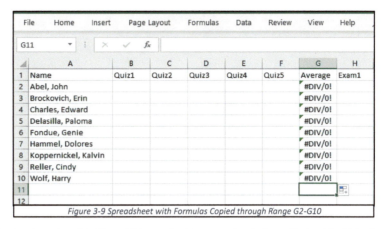

Figure 3-9 Spreadsheet with Formulas Copied through Range G2-G10

Although the function (AVERAGE) is copied into each of the cells in G2-G10, the range of values will change for each copy to reflect the row of values for which it is to compute the average. The copy of the formula in cell G3, for example, will calculate the average of numbers from B3 through F3

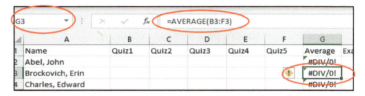

While that in cell B5 will calculate the average of numbers from B5 through F5.

When a function references (the contents of) cells by their Column-Row identifications, then a *copy* of that function references cells with Column-Row identifications adjusted according to the position of the new copy of the function. In the case of the quizzes, the original AVERAGE function in cell G2 references other cells in row 2, the copy in cell G3 will reference cells in row 3, the copy in G4 references cells in row 4, etc.

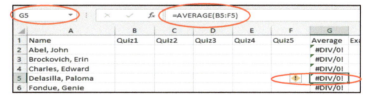

The professor will, of course, want to calculate the averages of the exams as well as those of the quizzes, so we will have to go through the same process for column L

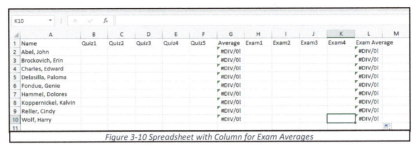

Figure 3-10 Spreadsheet with Column for Exam Averages

The professor might well be interested in the relative difficulty of his quizzes, and so would want to calculate the average scores in each of the individual quizzes. To calculate these, we might begin by entering a label (Quiz Average) in Cell A12, and then, with cell B12 selected, we once again select the AVERAGE function. Next we would place the cursor on cell B2, press the left mouse button and drag the cursor down to B10.

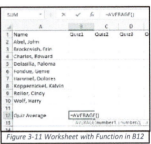

Figure 3-11 Worksheet with Function in B12

This structures the spreadsheet to calculate the average scores of the quiz 1. Now we place cursor on the dot on lower right corner of B12, press left mouse button and drag to F12, to copy the AVERAGE function into the cells B12 – F12.

The new copies of the AVERAGE function will have column identifications adjusted, just as the row numbers were adjusted when we copied the functions calculating student quiz averages into new rows (see Figure 3-13).

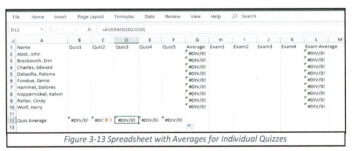

Figure 3-12 Worksheet with cells B2-B10 Selected

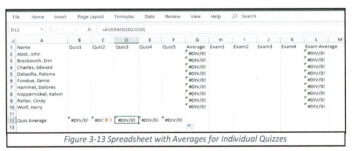

Figure 3-13 Spreadsheet with Averages for Individual Quizzes

3.1.7 Structuring the Spreadsheet for the Class: Inserting a User Defined Function

Assuming that the professor in the course has announced that the quiz average will count as 10% of the final grade in the course and the exam average will be counted 90% of the final score, he would now like to have a function to compute these final course grades.

There is, of course, no "built-in" function that will calculate 10% plus 90%, so we will have to create one.

We select a column for the course average (Column N) and enter an appropriate label at the top (in cell N1). Then, in the cell below it (cell N2), we enter the symbol = followed by the formula *0.1*G2+0.9*L2*

Notice that, as we enter the text in cell N2, it also appears in the formula bar.

When the content of a cell begins with the = symbol, what follow will be a formula/function and the value it produces when evaluated is what will be displayed in that cell. (Please note that in each of our AVERAGE functions, the first symbol in the cell is the = symbol)

In such a formula/function, the numbers from other cells are referenced using the column-row identifications of the cells and the arithmetic operations are identified using the following symbols:

- \+   indicates addition
- \-   indicates subtraction
- *   indicates multiplication
- /   indicates division

In the above example, a function was created (the entry begins with the symbol =) The function multiplies the number displayed in cell G2 by 0.1 (calculating 10% of John Abel's quiz average) and multiplies the number displayed in cell L2 by 0.9 (calculating 90% of his exam average) and adds the two products.

Click on the "Enter" check mark [× ✓ *fx*] to confirm the entry in L2

Now we put the mouse cursor on the dot at lower right corner of the N2 cell, press the left mouse button and drag down to cell N10 to copy the function into the rows corresponding to the other students (with appropriate adjustments to cell references in the formulas[11].)

---

[11]   Copying formulas by dragging downwards will produce increasing row numbers in the copies of the formulas. Dragging to the right will cause column references to increase (A to B, B to C, etc.) If you want a specific row and or column to be referenced in each copy of the formula, then placing a $ symbol to the left of the reference will lock the value so that it will not be adjusted when copying.
Example: All copies of the formula =$B3+$F3 will reference entries in column B and F (but different row numbers) and copies of the formula =B$3 + F$3 will reference entries in row 3

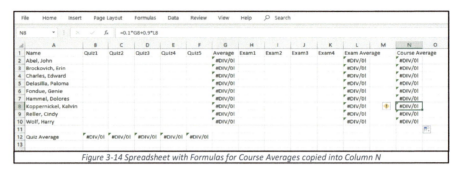

Figure 3-14 Spreadsheet with Formulas for Course Averages copied into Column N

After the professor has entered quiz and exam grades, the spreadsheet might look something like Figure 3-15 below.

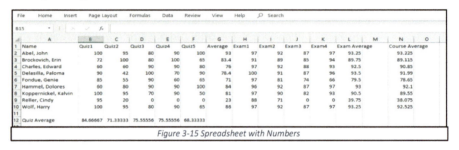

Figure 3-15 Spreadsheet with Numbers

3.1.8 Saving the Spreadsheet

The process of saving an Excel spreadsheet is essentially the same as that of saving a Word document.

If the spreadsheet has been saved previously, and we were saving a revised copy (with the same filename) then we would only have to click on the "Save" icon ⊞ in the upper left corner of the screen.

If, on the other hand, the spreadsheet has never been saved (or if we want to save the current version with a new name to differentiate it from earlier versions) then we begin by

clicking on the "File" tab in the upper left corner ⬚ and, in the left hand column in the window that opens, select "Save As"

From the "Save As" window you can navigate to a directory where you want to save the

new file (clicking on the "Browse" icon ⬚ Browse) and then enter the desired file

name in the "File Name" entry box. (see Figure 3-16)

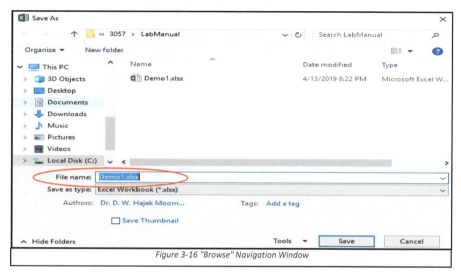

Figure 3-16 "Browse" Navigation Window

3.1.9 Exercises

3.1.9.1 Create a "shopping list" spreadsheet, with, in one column a list of items to be
purchased in another column, the number of the items purchased, in a third column
the price[12] per unit of each item, and in a fourth the total amount spent on that item
(computed with a user defined function). At the bottom of this column should be the
total bill.

(This kind of spreadsheet might be installed on a mobile device, and the user could fill
in item names, numbers and prices while shopping, and it could compute what his/her
bill should be before arriving at the cashier.).

---

[12] To display the number in a cell with a currency format (as a number of dollars and cents)

select that cell and click the $ symbol in the "Home" ribbon.

3.1.9.2 A car dealership sells several different models of cars. All cars of a given model have the same value/price.

Create a spreadsheet for the dealership, showing in one column, the names of the models, in another column the values of the models, in a third column the number of cars of each model currently on hand at the dealership, in yet another column the total value of all the cars available of the given model, and in still another column the number of recent sales of cars of that model. There should also be a column with the total values of recent sales of cars of the models. Finally, in a row beneath all of that, the spreadsheet should show total value of all cars on hand and the total value of all recent sales.

3.1.9.3 Create a spreadsheet that would calculate the "Grade Point Average" for a student.

In one column would be listed the courses that the student took. In a second column the number of credits of each course, and at the bottom, the total number of credits in all courses. In a third column his/her grade (numerical) in each course. In a fourth column the product of grade and credit value for each course, and at the bottom, the sum of all of those products. Finally, in another cell (labelled GPA) the quotient, the sum of the product sum divided by the sum of the credits.

3.2 Reformatting an Excel Project

The Excel spreadsheet we created in project 3.1 calculates and displays the desired values, but it doesn't make it easy for the viewer to distinguish between the computed averages and the individual quiz/exam scores.

Excel provides a number of facilities for making spreadsheets look better and convey information more effectively.

3.2.1 Representation of Decimal Values

Notice that the values computed as "averages" in the example spreadsheet appear with widely varying numbers of decimal digits, some with none, some with one digit, some with two, even some with 5 digits. The spreadsheet would look better if the decimal formats were more consistent.

One single decimal place would probably be appropriate for displaying quiz averages.

To achieve a uniform display format, we begin by selecting the cells with the quiz averages, and then clicking on the "Decrease Decimal" icon

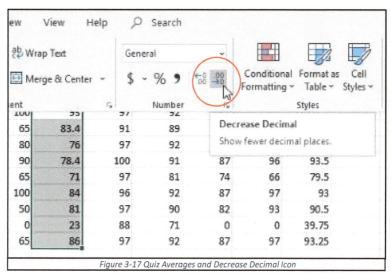

Figure 3-17 Quiz Averages and Decrease Decimal Icon

This will reformat the entries to the decimal display with common formatting (in this case no decimal digits.) Then, if we click on the "Increase Decimal" icon, we can set the display in each of the cells to one decimal digit. (Figure 3.18)

We can follow a similar process to adjust the decimal digits displayed in displays of the exam averages course averages and the quiz average display at bottom of the display. (Figure 3.19)

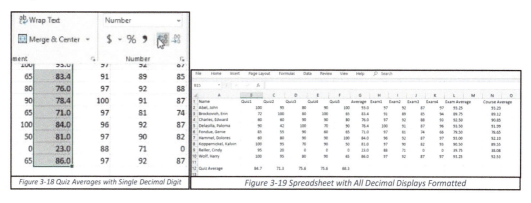

Figure 3-18 Quiz Averages with Single Decimal Digit   *Figure 3-19 Spreadsheet with All Decimal Displays Formatted*

3.2.2 Alignment of Cell Displays, Separation and Widths of Columns

The spreadsheet displays all of the numerical values in columns of the same width and, with the exception of the Course Average column, in columns that are adjacent. Because they are so close together, it is difficult to distinguish different types of information.

It seems reasonable for the data for exams to be separated from that of the quizzes. We can do that by selecting a cell in the Exam 1 column, then clicking on the "Insert" icon in the "Home" ribbon and select "Insert Sheet Columns" from the dropdown menu.

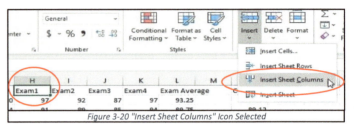

Figure 3-20 "Insert Sheet Columns" Icon Selected

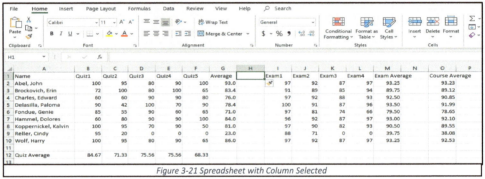

Figure 3-21 Spreadsheet with Column Selected

The labels in the headings over the columns with numerical values do not align well with the numbers. The numbers are "right aligned" while the labels are left aligned.

We can change the label alignment by first selecting the labels, and then clicking on the "Right Align" icon

Figure 3-22 Pointing to "Right Align" Icon

The result is pretty good, except for columns L and M where the M column is not wide enough to hold the entire label.

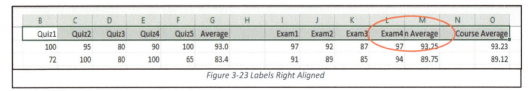

Figure 3-23 Labels Right Aligned

To fix this problem, we place the cursor at the right edge of the "M" cell and press the left mouse button. The cursor changes to a double arrow ✛ . Then we drag the edge to the right, enlarging the column to the point that the labels do not interfere with each other.

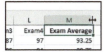

3.2.3 Chart Displaying Data

To help a user visualize data in a spreadsheet, Excel provides many sophisticated tools to create graphic displays for data representation.

In this situation of this example, the professor might be interested in a display to illustrate the relative difficulty of the quizzes.

We could start by selecting the data to be represented (the quiz score averages.)

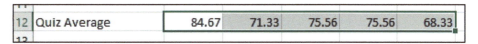

Then we would click on the little square on lower right hand corner of the selected range, and the *quick analysis tool* opens

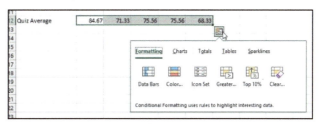

For this project we want to click the "*Charts*" tab and several different kind of chart options will be displayed.

When we choose one of the options, that kind of chart will open, displaying the selected data (in this case, the quiz averages)

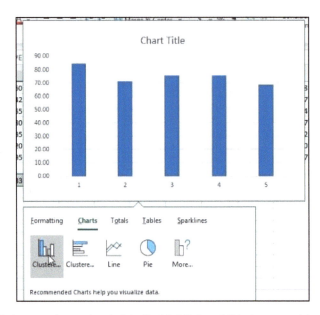

The bars, in this bar graph are simply labelled 1,2,3,4 and 5 but we would prefer they be labelled to identify the data they represent.

Now we select the labels at the top of the columns and copy them to the clipboard.

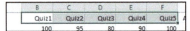

Then we open the chart label field and paste the copied labels.

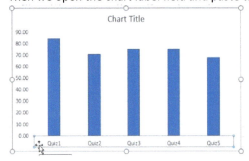

We can also edit the "Chart Title" and position the graph on the page (click on graph to "select" it and drag to the desired location. Figure 3.24)

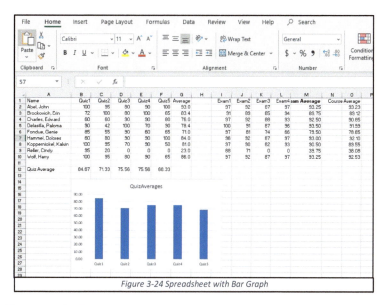

Figure 3-24 Spreadsheet with Bar Graph

3.2.4 Help Features in Excel

The Microsoft Excel tabs include two help features, the "Search" tab and the "Help" tab (very similar to those in Word.)

Just as in Word, you can also get help by pressing the F1 key.

3.2.4.1 The Search Tab

If you click on the "Search" tab ⟨ 🔍 Search ⟩ (or press Alt Q) a small window will open

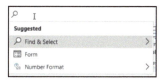

It has a line (to the right of the 🔍 icon) where you can enter a description of what you want information/help about. As you type your entry, suggestions below the line will change while you type, as the system keeps trying to "guess" what it is you might be entering.

Of course the suggestions will be appropriate to Excel, rather than Word.

3.2.4.2 The Help Tab

If you click on the "Help" tab,
the "Help" ribbon (very similar
to that of the Word "Help"
ribbon) will display

Clicking on the Help icon

 in the ribbon will
open the "Help column"
on the right of the screen
where you can enter
whatever it is you want
information about.

3.2.5 Exercises

3.2.5.1 Create a spreadsheet showing: in one column the names of (at least 4) baseball teams, in a second column the number of games played by the teams, in another column the number of runs scored by the teams, and in yet another column the number of runs scored per game by the teams (expressed with three decimal digits of accuracy.)
Below the numbers there should be a graph showing the runs per game for the teams.

3.2.5.2 A car dealership sells several different models of cars. All cars of a given model have the same value/price. Create a spreadsheet for the dealership, showing in one row, the names of (at least 4) car models (do not put a model name in column 1.)
In row 2, under each model name should be the price of that model.

Below the model/price display should be: In column A, a list of the names of (at least 4) salesmen.
In the column for each model, in the row for each salesman should be a the number of sales of that model of car by that salesman.
In the column to the right of the last car model should be the total values of the sales for that salesman. There should also be a graph displaying the total value of sales by each salesman.

3.2.5.3 Create a "shopping list" spreadsheet. Along the top row should be a list of recipes. Down the left column should be a list of items to be purchased.
In the row for an item, under each recipe should be the number of units of the item needed for the recipe. Then, to the right of the recipe entries should be an entry for the price per unit of the item, and another entry for the total amount to be spent on that item.
In a row beneath all of the items should be entries for the total amount to be spent on the recipe of each column.
Finally there should be two graphs, one displaying the cost of the recipes and the other showing the amounts spent on the items.

Chapter 4 Presentation Programs

A **presentation program** is a software package used to display information in the form of a "*slide show*".

Presentations like this are widely used in business communications, (especially in business planning) as well as in education and, generally, anywhere ideas are to be communicated. Presentations may also feature prominently in political settings where persuasion is a central motivating issue.

A presentation program is supposed to help both the speaker and the participants/viewers. It will provide visual information which complements the talk. There are many different types of presentations including professional (work-related), education, entertainment, and for general communication.

The presentation program included in the Microsoft Office software suite is called PowerPoint and is probably the best known of all the presentation programs (to the point the name "PowerPoint" is often used as a generic term for "presentation program".)

4.1 Opening a Project with Microsoft PowerPoint

To start a PowerPoint project, we begin by (double) clicking on the PowerPoint Icon to open the PowerPoint "Home" window.

4.1.1 PowerPoint "Home" Window

Figure 4-1 PowerPoint "Home" Window

The *Home* window provides several icons:

One for initiating a new PowerPoint project  ,
and a few for tutorials/wizards for new users

There is also a list of recent PowerPoint projects

Recent   Pinned   Shared with Me

	Name	Date modified
	ComputerGraphicsAppendix4BWithTopiQuizzes.pptx C: » a-databak » coursedevelopement » 4046 » Jan2019 » LecturePowerpoints	Yesterday at 5:09 PM
	LecturesProgLang13.pptx	Yesterday at 9:02 AM

4.1.2 PowerPoint "Open" Window

In the left hand column of the "Home" window, the [Open] icon provides access to more
sophisticated tools for finding and opening existing projects:

Figure 4-2 PowerPoint Open Window

4.1.3 PowerPoint "New" Window

The 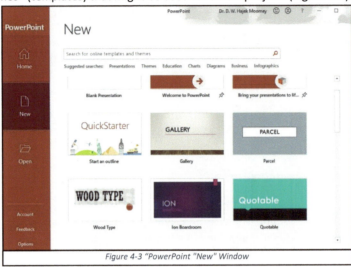 icon in the left hand column gives access to a number of preprogrammed visual "Themes" (templates) that might be used for a new project: (Figure 4.3)

Figure 4-3 "PowerPoint "New" Window

4.1.4 Initiating the Project

A professor might want to create a sequence of PowerPoint slides to supplement his lecture on the first day of a class.

If we click on one of the "Blank Presentation icons 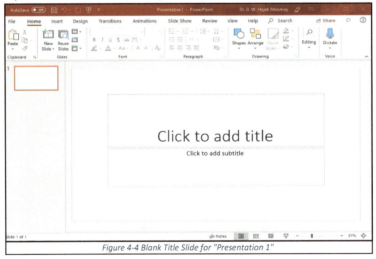 a "Presentation" will open (default title "Presentation 1")
It will display a "blank" title slide (see Figure 4-4)

Figure 4-4 Blank Title Slide for "Presentation 1"

4.1.5 Title Slide

The title slide will be the first slide displayed in the presentation, and our professor would probably use it to identify the course he would be talking about. He/we would enter this information where the slide says "Click to add title" and "Click to add subtitle. After course title, etc. have been entered, we can check what the resulting slide would look like by clicking on the "Reading View" icon at the bottom of the display.

Figure 4-5 Title Slide with Information Entered

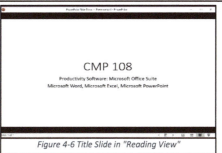

Figure 4-6 Title Slide in "Reading View"

(We would return to the "Normal" or "Editing" view by clicking on the "Normal" icon at the bottom of the display.)

The display might look better if the first line in the "Subtitle" block were slightly larger. We can accomplish this by selecting the line and adjusting the "Font Size" in the "Font" block of the "Home" ribbon.

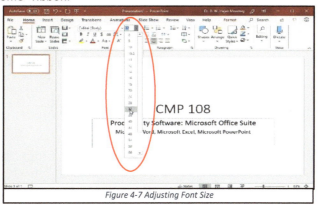

Figure 4-7 Adjusting Font Size

4.1.6 Outline of Lecture

Recall that this "Slideshow" (like most) will be displayed as the professor talks. It should show points of emphasis and details that should be remembered. It would *not* be a word for word repetition of what he will be saying. (Nor should the professor simply read aloud what is displayed.)

4.1.6.1 Content of First Day Lecture

The professor will probably begin by introducing himself.

Next, he would give a brief general outline of the course

Then a very brief description of each of the primary topics of the course (in this example:Microsoft Word, Excel and PowerPoint.)

4.1.7 Slide for Professor Introduction

Our project will first need a slide to supplement the professor's self introduction:

We click on the "New Slide" icon in the "Home" Ribbon  and a menu appears showing several slide format options.
(Probably the most commonly used option is the "Title and Content" format.)

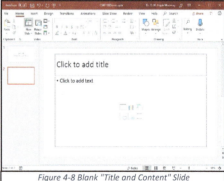

Figure 4-8 Blank "Title and Content" Slide

We would enter an appropriate "Title" for a first slide in a presentation:

Professor in Charge of CMP 108

Next we consider the "Content" block. In this block of the default title slide, entries will be displayed using a "Bullet" format:

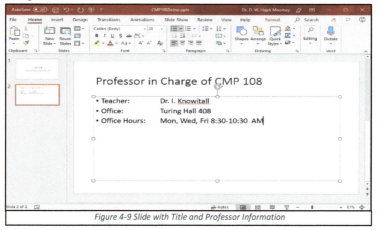

Figure 4-9 Slide with Title and Professor Information

4.1.8 Slide for Course Description

An alternative method for inserting a new slide is to right click on a left column slide icon, and then selecting the "New Slide" option from the resulting menu.

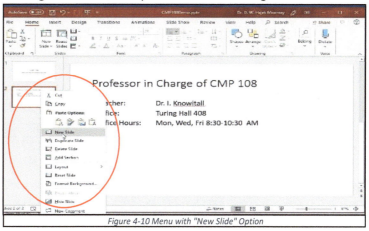

Figure 4-10 Menu with "New Slide" Option

This inserts a new slide with the same format as that of the slide that was right clicked (in this case, the "Title and Content" format.)

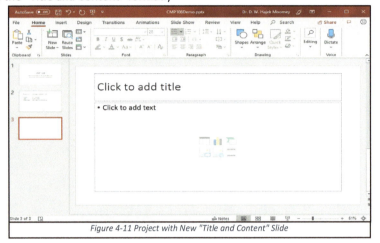

Figure 4-11 Project with New "Title and Content" Slide

The entries in "Bullet" format can be inset using the tab key (normally the key marked "→")

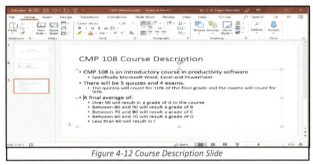

Figure 4-12 Course Description Slide

4.1.8 Slides for Course Content

The lecture would also include a short description of each of the Microsoft Office programs to be studied: Word, Excel and PowerPoint. Each would have its own slide, and each of the slides would be created the same way that the "Course Description" slide was created; right click on an icon in the left column and select "New Slide" from the dropdown menu, then edit the resulting slide.

Figure 4-13 Slides for Word, Excel and PowerPoint

4.1.9 Slide with Image

It seems reasonable that the professor should also tell the students what the textbook for the course is. He would do this with a slide immediately following the one with the course description.

Select that slide and then click on the "New Slide" icon from the "Home" ribbon. (We do this rather than right clicking the slide identifier in the left column because we will use a different slide format.)

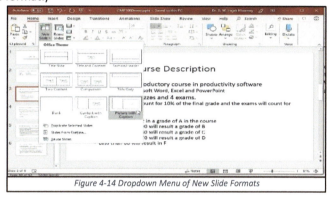

Figure 4-14 Dropdown Menu of New Slide Formats

Choose the "Picture with Caption" option from the dropdown menu.

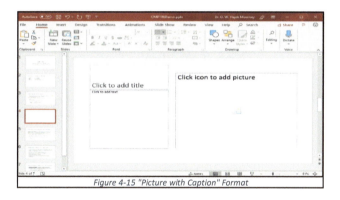

Figure 4-15 "Picture with Caption" Format

We can enter an image by clicking on the icon and navigating to a directory with the desired image.

When we select the image, PowerPoint will provide several alternative design alternatives.

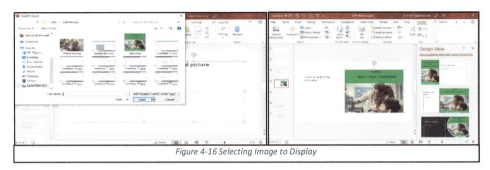

Figure 4-16 Selecting Image to Display

After selecting a display alternative, we can enter the text description of the textbook.

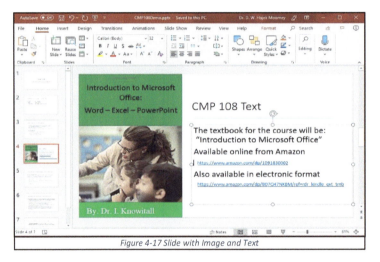

Figure 4-17 Slide with Image and Text

4.1.10 Applying a Theme

The professor's presentation is complete, but it is a little bland and colorless. It is all black text on white background[13].

PowerPoint provides a number of "Themes" that can be applied to the slideshow, adding elements of color, and making the presentation more interesting.

The themes can be found in the ribbon under the "Design" tab

Figure 4-18 Design Ribbon showing Theme Options

---

[13]   With the exception of the textbook illustration, of course.

Clicking on one of the "Theme" options will apply the formatting style to all of the slides in the presentation.

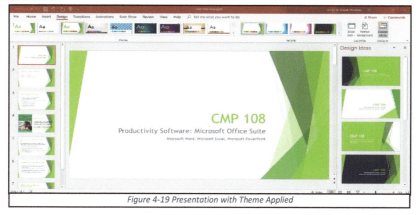

Figure 4-19 Presentation with Theme Applied

4.1.11 Extra Design Ideas

After choosing a theme, there will be a number of alternative "Design Ideas" which can be applied to individual slides. (If the "Design Ideas" do not appear in a column at the right of

the editing area, you can open it by clicking on the "Design Ideas" icon located at the right of the "Design" ribbon.

We can apply one of these designs to a slide by first selecting the slide, and then clicking on the design we want applied to that slide.

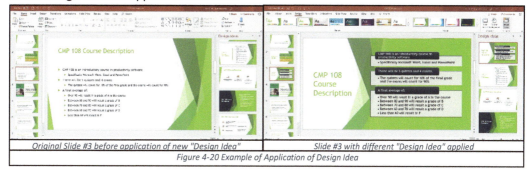

Original Slide #3 before application of new "Design Idea"   *Slide #3 with different "Design Idea" applied*

Figure 4-20 Example of Application of Design Idea

4.1.12 Exercises

4.1.12.1 Create a presentation similar to that in the example above for a course that you are familiar with. The presentation should have at least 5 slides. The teacher's self introduction page should include an image, a picture of the teacher. (This is *presumably* a *fictional* course with a *fictional* teacher, so do not feel constrained by the truth, just by laws governing libel and defamation of character.) The presentation should have a colored theme applied (as in the above project) and it should utilize at least one "Design Idea".

4.1.12.2 Create a presentation that a (fictional) salesman might use in promoting the sales of vacation packages. The presentation should have at least 5 slides, it should have a colored theme applied (as above) and it should utilize at least one "Design Idea".

4.1.12.3 Create a presentation that will explain/show how to prepare a dish like ZucchiniSpaghetti (see Chapter 1)

4.2 Dynamic PowerPoint Presentations

The slide show developed in the previous section has a simple display format. Every time the presenter clicks his/her mouse button or presses a key, the current slide immediately disappears, and is replaced by the next slide (in its entirety.)

This is kind of transition is quite adequate for a short sequence like the example, but for a longer lecture with numerous slides, it can become boring.

PowerPoint provides a number of techniques for making the presentation more dynamic and helping keep the audience awake and interested.

4.2.1 Transitions

The "Transitions" tab gives us a number of options for "transitioning" from one slide to the next.

Figure 4-21 Default "Transitions" Ribbon

These provide a wide range of visual effects as the display changes from that of one slide to the next.

A "Transition" effect is applied to a slide by simply clicking on the effect icon while the slide is in the editing window.

If, with slide #2 showing in the editing window, we click the "Push" icon [Push] and set "Effect Options" to "From the Right" [Effect Options] then the transition from slide #1 to #2 will proceed as shown in Figure 4-22 below.

Figure 4-22 Transitioning from slide 1 to slide 2 using "Push" from Right

Although the default "Transitions" ribbon shows what are probably the most popular transitions, there are many more.

Clicking on the "More" icon at the right of the display will open a larger selection of Transitions options (see Figure 4-23.)

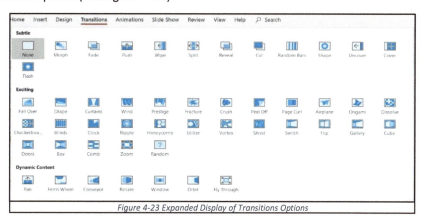

Figure 4-23 Expanded Display of Transitions Options

4.2.2 Animations

Now we have some (hopefully) interesting visual effects as presentation transitions from one slide to another.

PowerPoint also provides tools to support additional "Animations" once a slide is displayed.

Possibly the most common use of these "Animations" is to display objects one at a time as the presenter talks about each of them in turn.

Dr. Knowitall might, for example, feel that, when discussing the "Creating, editing, saving and printing documents" aspect of Microsoft Word (the first entry in the list of functions provided) it would be distracting to have the lines concerning "Copying ...", "Formatting ...", etc. on the screen too. He would like to talk about one

set of functions, then have another line appear so he could talk about those functions, then have another line appear so he could talk about its functions, and so on.

4.2.2.1 Starting the Animation

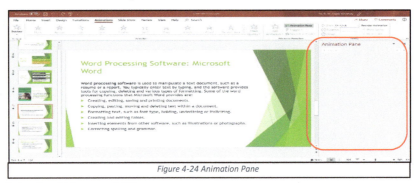

If we click on the "Animation Pane" icon the "Animation Pane" will appear in a column on the right of the window.

Figure 4-24 Animation Pane

4.2.2.2 Selecting Objects and Effects

Next, select the "objects" that we want to "animate"

(the six bulleted lines)

Now choose an animation effect (we will choose "Appear" for this example) and icons representing each of the selected objects will appear in the animation pane.

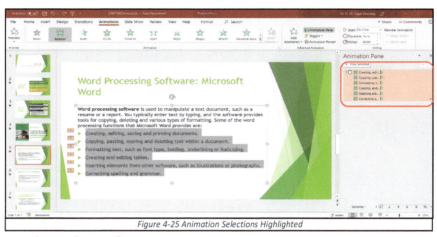

Figure 4-25 Animation Selections Highlighted

4.2.2.3 Applying a "Trigger"

Clicking on the lower right corner of the selection section opens a list of options for

triggering the animation effect.

We select the "Start on Click" option  (probably the most commonly used trigger option.) This will apply the "Appear" animation triggered by the click of the mouse button to each of the selected objects.

Figure 4-26 Slide 5 With All lines Animated to "Appear" After a Mouse Click

4.2.2.4 Animated Slide

When the professor's lecture comes to slide 5, each time he clicks his mouse button, a new line will "Appear" on the screen.

| Initial display | After One Click | After Second Click | After Third Click |

Figure 4-27 Display Sequence of Slide 5

The animation effects are triggered in the order in which they appear in the Animation Pane, not by the position on the display screen.

4.2.2.5 Extra Effects

The animation effects displayed in the default "Animation" ribbon are not the only ones available.

Clicking on the "More" icon at the right of the "Animation" ribbon will open a window (Figure 4-28) displaying a wider range of animation effects, including effects for removing/hiding elements from the display, for moving them from one place to another and for simply attracting the viewers' attention.

Figure 4-28 Additional "Animation" Effects

Note that there are even more effects available by clicking icons at the bottom of the window.

4.2.3 Extra Commentary

We note that PowerPoint also provides | Help   🔍 Search | tabs that work much as they do in Word and Excel.

The function of PowerPoint is usually to *supplement* a presentation, not to *be* the presentation. Excessive use of animations, transitions and/or "Design Ideas" can easily distract from the presentation

4.2.4 Exercises

4.2.4.1 Create a presentation similar to that in the example in the text for a course that you are familiar with. The presentation should have at least 5 slides.
The teacher's self introduction page should include an image, a picture of the teacher.
As in Exercise 4.1.12.1, this is *presumably* a *fictional* course with a *fictional* teacher. You need not feel constrained considerations of reality. (You should, however, take into consideration copyright laws, as well as those governing libel and defamation of character.)
The image of the teacher should "Float" into view upon the first mouse click. .

4.2.4.2 Create a presentation that a (fictional) used car salesman might use. The presentation should have at least 5 slides, each describing a different car, its features, price and financing terms. The different elements of the slides should be "Animated" to display

4.2.4.3 Create a presentation that will explain/show how to bake a cake. Use "animation" to emphasize the sequence in which the different steps must be carried out.

Chapter 5 Microsoft Paint

Microsoft Paint has been included with almost all versions of Microsoft Windows since its first release. It is also sometimes referred to as **MS Paint** as well as **Microsoft Paint**. The program opens and saves files with Windows bitmap format (24-bit, 256 color, 16 color, and monochrome, all with the .bmp extension.) It also supports JPEG, GIF (without animation or transparency), PNG and TIFF. Paint does not, however, support grayscale.

Because various versions of Paint have been provided over the years, much of the above (and below) might have a somewhat different appearance when you try it on your computer (especially if you are using a version different than the one used for this example.)

Because of its simplicity (and widespread availability), Paint very quickly became one of the most popular applications in the early versions of Windows — introducing many beginning users to computer graphics.

Its simplicity also makes it an excellent choice for relatively simple graphics projects. It is easily available, loads quickly, requires relatively few resources, and has a relatively simple (and user friendly) user interface.

In this project, we will create a graphic image similar to Figure 1 here.

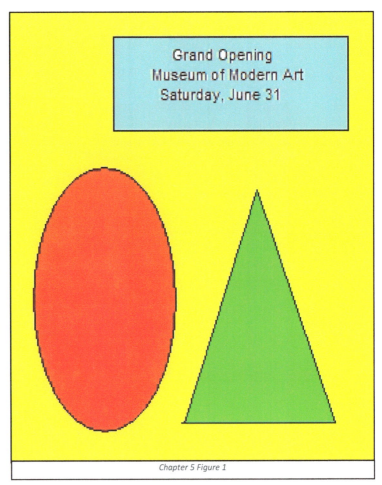

Chapter 5 Figure 1

5.1 Opening the program

We begin by locating the icon for the Paint program.

Then we click on it to open the program.

When the program opens, we should see something like the image in Figure 3.

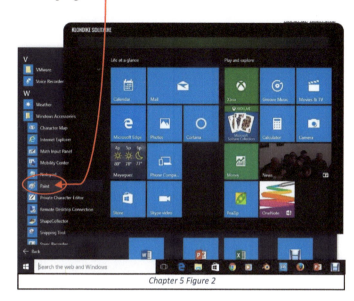

Chapter 5 Figure 2

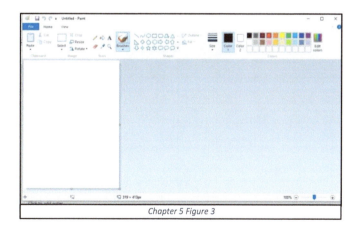

Chapter 5 Figure 3

5.2 Page setup

It seems reasonable that our project might be designed to be printed on standard 8.5×11 inch paper.

Click on the "File" tab
in the upper left corner of the screen as shown in Figure 4

Then place the cursor over "Print" in the drop-down menu (Figure 5)

On the submenu that opens, click on "Page Setup" (Figure 6)

The Page setup menu opens. (Figure 7)
make sure that:

Paper size is set to Letter

Orientation is set to Portrait

All margins are set to 0.5 inches

Click on "OK"

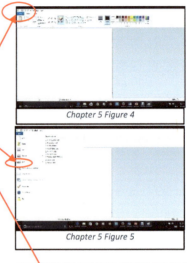

Chapter 5 Figure 4

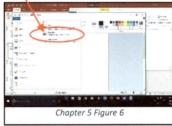

Chapter 5 Figure 5

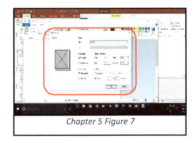

Chapter 5 Figure 6

Chapter 5 Figure 7

5.3 Properties

Click on "File" again and this time, select "Properties" (Figure 8)

The "Image Properties" dialog box opens (Figure 9)

In the "Image Properties" dialog box:

set Units to "Inches"

Our paper will be 8.5×11 inches, but, on the Page Setup men
we specified margins of .5 inches.

Set Width to 7.50 and Height to 10

Make sure that "Color" is checked

Click on OK

If necessary zoom in or out for proper size of display. So that
the
entire picture fits on the screen, but the scale makes the
design easy to discern. (as in Figure 10)

5.4 Background Color

We wanted the background of our announcement to be yellow,
not white.

click on "Color 1", then click on the yellow color in the color disp

click on the *"fill with color"* icon (Figure 12)

move the cursor into the paint area and click

the color of the area will change from white to yellow
(as in Figure 13)

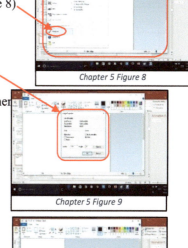

Chapter 5 Figure 8

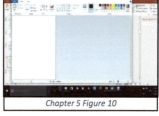

Chapter 5 Figure 9

Chapter 5 Figure 10

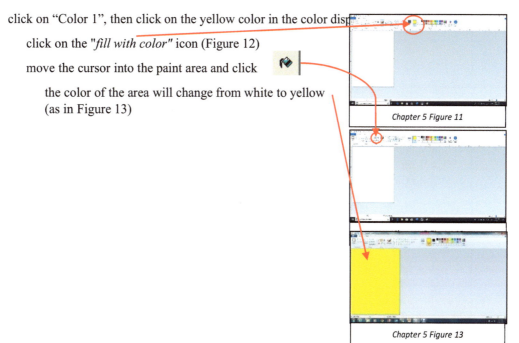

Chapter 5 Figure 11

Chapter 5 Figure 13

5.5 Red Oval

Our project calls for a red oval with a black border

Select the ***ellipse*** *shape icon*
*(*See Figure 14*)*

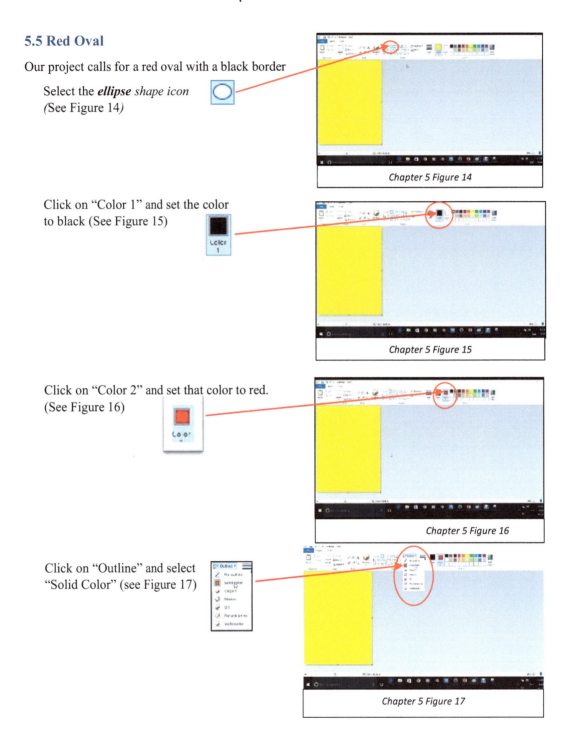

Chapter 5 Figure 14

Click on "Color 1" and set the color
to black (See Figure 15)

Chapter 5 Figure 15

Click on "Color 2" and set that color to red.
(See Figure 16)

Chapter 5 Figure 16

Click on "Outline" and select
"Solid Color" (see Figure 17)

Chapter 5 Figure 17

5.6 Red Oval

Click on "Fill"
and select "Solid Color"
(See Figure 18)

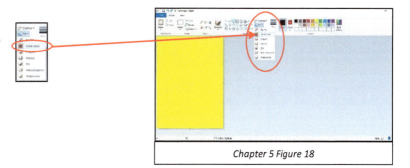

Chapter 5 Figure 18

Place the cursor at approximately (0.75×3.5 in)
    Notice that the position of the cursor is
    given at lower left corner (See Figure 19)

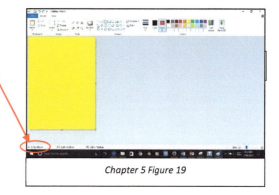

Chapter 5 Figure 19

Press the mouse button, drag the cursor to
approximately 3.75×9.5 in and release the button
(The display should look like Figure 20)

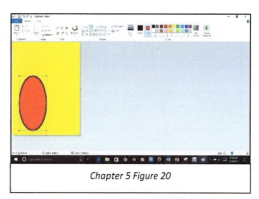

Chapter 5 Figure 20

5.7 Green Triangle

Next, we select the triangle icon
(See Figure 21)

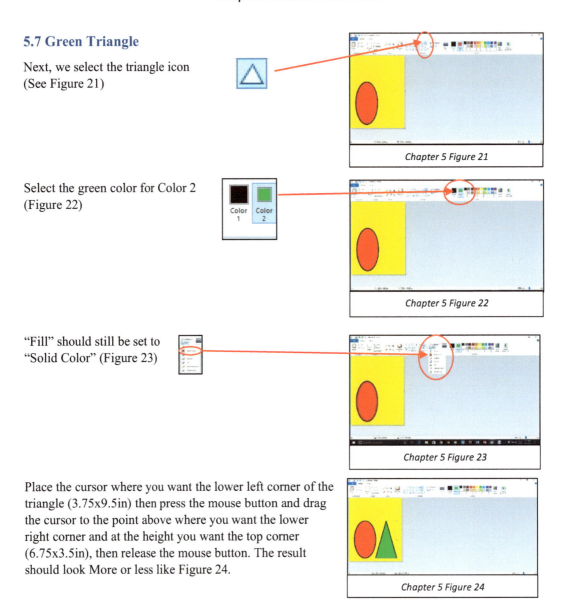

Select the green color for Color 2
(Figure 22)

"Fill" should still be set to
"Solid Color" (Figure 23)

Place the cursor where you want the lower left corner of the
triangle (3.75x9.5in) then press the mouse button and drag
the cursor to the point above where you want the lower
right corner and at the height you want the top corner
(6.75x3.5in), then release the mouse button. The result
should look More or less like Figure 24.

Chapter 5 Figure 21

Chapter 5 Figure 22

Chapter 5 Figure 23

Chapter 5 Figure 24

5.8 Box for Text

Now we want to display some text,
but first we need a box in which to insert the text.

In our assigned project (Figure 1), the border of
the box is black, so Color 1 should be black

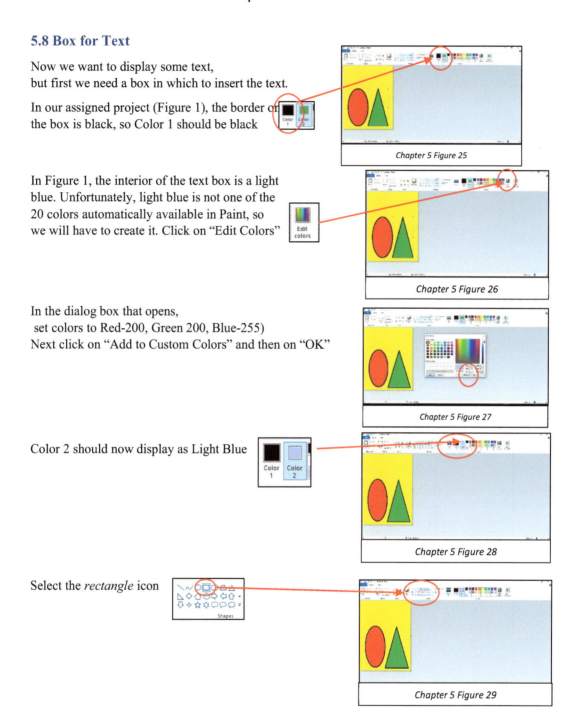

Chapter 5 Figure 25

In Figure 1, the interior of the text box is a light
blue. Unfortunately, light blue is not one of the
20 colors automatically available in Paint, so
we will have to create it. Click on "Edit Colors"

Chapter 5 Figure 26

In the dialog box that opens,
 set colors to Red-200, Green 200, Blue-255)
Next click on "Add to Custom Colors" and then on "OK"

Chapter 5 Figure 27

Color 2 should now display as Light Blue

Chapter 5 Figure 28

Select the *rectangle* icon

Chapter 5 Figure 29

5.9 Box for Text

Place the cursor where you want the upper left corner of the box to be (2.5, 0.5 in.), then click and drag the cursor to where you want the lower right corner of the box to be (6.75, 3.0 in.) then release the mouse button. The result should look like Figure 30.

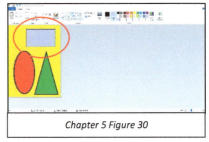

Chapter 5 Figure 30

Next, we have to add the text.
Click on the *text* icon (the letter A in the Tools

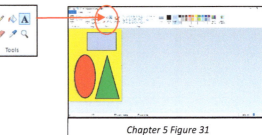

Chapter 5 Figure 31

Now we select a rectangle where the text will be displayed
Place the cursor in the upper left corner of the rectangle, press the mouse button and drag to the lower right corner and release the button. A dotted line appears around the rectangle and the ribbon display changes to a text display

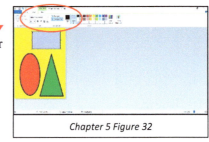

Chapter 5 Figure 32

Select a font (Times New Roman) Font size (24) Font style (Bold) and background (Transparent). Then enter the text in the dotted rectangle

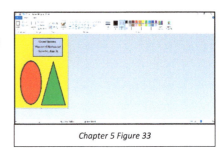

Chapter 5 Figure 33

Chapter 5 Questions

Appendix 1 Questions 1 True-False

1.1 Microsoft Paint does not support grayscale.

1.2 To draw an oval in our graphic, we press the left mouse button, drag the cursor around the shape of the oval we want displayed.

1.3 When drawing an oval in our graphic, the interior will be filled with the color selected in the "Color 2" icon

1.4 To draw a triangle in our graphic, we press the left mouse button, drag the cursor from the lower left hand corner of the rectangle containing the triangle up to the position for the top vertex of the triangle.

1-5 If we want or need a color that is not available in Microsoft Paint's default collection of 20 colors, we can click on "Edit Colors" In the dialog box that opens we can define our new color by specifying integer values between 0 and 255 for red, green and blue components.

Appendix 1 Questions 2 Multiple Choice

2-1 Microsoft Paint _____ and requires relatively few resources
   a. is easily available
   b. loads quickly
   c. requires relatively few resources
   d. all of the above|
   e. none of the above

2-2 In Microsoft Paint, in the Page Setup dialog box we can select the document's _____
   a. paper size
   b. orientation
   c. margin size
   d. all of the above
   e. none of the above

2-3 In Microsoft Paint, we can control the document's orientation in the _____ dialog box
   a. Page Setup
   b. Print
   c. Properties
   d. Image Properties
   e. none of the above

2-4 In Microsoft Paint, we can control the document's file type in the _____ dialog box
   a. Page Setup
   b. Print
   c. Properties
   d. Image Properties
   e. none of the above

Appendix 1 Questions 3 Completion

3-1 In the "_____ Properties" dialog box we can set Units to Inches.

3-2 When we need a color that is not available in the default selection, we click on "Edit Colors", select values for the red, green and blue components, then click on "Add to _____ Colors" and then on "OK